REIKI
 a beginner's guide

D1321985

SANDI LEIR SHUFFREY

Hodder & Stoughton
A MEMBER OF THE HODDER HEADLINE GROUP

Dedication and acknowledgement

To my children Kim and Tallis who are my Saving Graces; Ma and Pa who support me no matter what; to Jane, teacher in absentia; to Carolyn Finlay who keeps me on 'the other side' where I belong; to Penny Prince and Susie Trotter for being my loyal friends without judgement; to Sue Kay and the Ravenscrofts for creating the space; to Angela Robertshaw for honouring me, my teaching and the Divine Laws; to Andy Halsey for being a mirror and leading me into the Shaman's Death; to David Hubbard whose incredible patience and skill helped me to keep hold of my Truth and create a new future; to Ethne, my Angel; to Teresa Moorey for giving me this opportunity; to Deborah Irving for the crash course in 'Word' and her patience; to Maharaji for taking away my darkness and giving me eternal light; to Wil Kay, may Reiki hold your soul until you see it clearly for yourself; to Nicky Van Gelder, let the magic become yours.

To all my students, for without the student there can be no Master.

Permission is acknowledged for the photographs of Masters from Phyllis Furomoto.

Order queries: please contact Bookpoint Ltd, 39 Milton Park, Abingdon, Oxon OX14 4TD. Telephone: (44) 01235 400414, Fax: (44) 01235 400454. Lines are open from 9.00 - 6.00, Monday to Saturday, with a 24 hour message answering service. Email address: orders@bookpoint.co.uk

British Library Cataloguing in Publication Data
A catalogue record for this title is available from The British Library

ISBN 0 340 72081 6

First published 1998
Impression number 10 9 8 7 6 5 4 3 2
Year   2003 2002 2001 2000

Typeset by Transet Limited, Coventry, England.
Printed in Great Britain for Hodder & Stoughton Educational, a division of Hodder Headline Plc, 338 Euston Road, London NW1 3BH by Cox and Wyman Limited, Reading, Berks.

CONTENTS

INTRODUCTION

Chinese Buddhist Symbol of Light – the symbol of spiritual knowledge and enlightenment

Materialism breeds boredom, boredom breeds inertia, inertia breeds loss of happiness, disease and eventually death.

Dr E. Bach

The word *Reiki* means Universal Life Energy: the energy within us and around us, the energy from which all things are made; a creative intelligence in unlimited supply.

In learning this simple, practical, hands-on technique we are able to tap into the reservoir of our unlimited potential. Through a process of initiation the unmanifest, unseen, becomes accessible to us, not only in understanding but also in a useful healing process.

In a two-day class, usually held over a weekend, students are given four initiations that show how to direct the energy through the hands into various areas of the body. Students learn how to give a full body treatment on others and receive a full body treatment from others to experience the Reiki in all ways. Instruction on self-treatment is also given and stressed as being very important. A knowledge of anatomy and physiology or diagnosis of illness is not necessary although it may help with later understanding.

To study Reiki nothing is required of you other than to be open-minded and willing to learn. You do not need to be a calm, caring person, or know anything in particular. If you have life force then you are able to receive Reiki. There is at least one person in every class who feels that he or she is the one who won't 'get it', but they always do, if taught correctly (see Chapter 7 on Finding a Master).

Full balance is restored sometimes gradually over several sessions, sometimes very rapidly. A sense of awakening occurs, a new way of seeing and living begins to evolve.

Reiki is not a religion, neither is it contradictory to any religion because by nature it is universal. Indeed, I have taught people from all paths, Buddhists, Christians, Muslims, Shamans, followers of Sai Baba, Muktanand, Guru Mai, Maharaji, Mother Meera, Maharishi, atheists and the best converts of all, sceptics. I have taught spiritual healers, mediums, clairvoyants and many ordinary people who may feel they know nothing. The common experience of all being that Reiki is a tangible method to deepen our understanding of what we already have.

In the form I teach there is no specific dogma, no need to be vegetarian or give anything up. Come as you are and see what can happen. No one can tell you how to live your life, they can advise, but ultimately you choose each direction and become responsible for the choices. The word 'responsibility' literally means the ability to respond. That, to me, is a flowing natural ability but not so easy to do as we judge our lives, actions and words through other people's expectations of us and become ill as a result.

The physical results of Reiki can be very surprising, as can the falling away of old habit patterns, even those passed down by our ancestors. New habits begin, the most important being the daily self-treatment by Reiki. Self-treatment is a thing many of us miss out on as we have been told to be less selfish and to become kind, giving people. How can we help others if we are sick and confused ourselves? How can we teach our children a way of being in balance if we have never experienced it for ourselves? How can we talk about God when God is a concept, a belief system and not an experience in our hearts, a knowing? We struggle on, we do our best but somewhere inside our head a voice always says 'Not good enough'.

Reiki restores the sense of self-worth. It gives back a sense of purpose, a way to remain centred and clear thinking; a way to prevent the accumulation of stress. It is used successfully for all manner of ills. To relieve pain, heal wounds, mend bones, bring about digestive balance, help combat food allergies and eating disorders, help relieve the side effects of medications and serious diseases such as diabetes, high blood pressure, cancer, etc. Not only does a physical healing take place but also a change in mental attitude and an emotional calming. Reiki heals the longing heart.

When I heard the word 'Reiki' I knew I had to reach out and grab it with both hands. I was totally unprepared for how far the change would take me.

In these chapters I shall describe how to learn Reiki, its application and potential and hopefully present to you an avenue of understanding and an opportunity to be inspired to go further.

First, come for yourself.

*We can learn to have choices about
what we are doing with our energy.*

Stuart Wilde, *The Force*

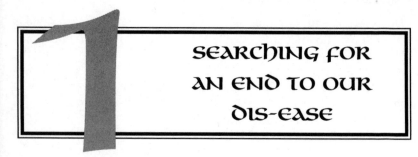

1

SEARChING FOR AN END TO OUR DIS-EASE

You know it's time to change when the pain of holding on is greater than the pain of letting go.

The NATURE OF ILLNESS

It is important to begin with an understanding of the nature of disease, for that is probably what has encouraged us to read a book on healing. At first, it seems a little abstract in form but gradually a picture emerges of how we may have become ill and how we can again become well – we have the power in our own hands. When we have a toothache we put our hand to our jaw and it seems to help; when our child has a stomach ache we gently rub it with our hand and it helps. It helps because life force is already within us in the form of energy. It constantly ebbs and flows into us and out of us.

Given the theory that we create our own illness then we can create our own well-being. This theory will be explained in this chapter.

Our bodies are created from the combined energies of our soul-self, emotional-self and mind-self. They are a reflection of our inner condition. We are not our bodies but our bodies are us. By the time the accumulation of stress and conflict creates an illness in the body it has been an illness in the energy system for some time but, as we are no longer familiar with our inner stillness and silence, we have not recognised it. The body is, therefore, screaming out at us by producing a physical condition: a headache, a joint pain, an ulcer, a tumour, a lung disease.

4

Illness comes about as a result of an interruption in our outward flow of energy. We are made up of feelings, needs and desires which reach out into the world, sometimes being met when all flows well, and sometimes being blocked with a conflict of ideas or others' desires for it to be different. We want our thoughts and desires to manifest a good life for us but the world needs to participate. As the world is full of diverse, unique people, agreement with us is not inevitable. Conflict with our energy flow can be useful as a means of gaining knowledge and understanding of ourselves and others, or it can cause great pain. The accumulation of pain begins to mask us from our original connection to our source, the energy of our creation. Only when we feel connected do we move forwards in balance. Sooner or later the disconnection causes an accumulation of stress. It begins as a negative energy level, unseen but quietly detectable by the feeling heart. By now, however, we have forgotten the language of the heart. So the next step our soul takes to re-awaken us to balance is to create from the imploding energy a block on the physical plane, i.e. the body.

The part affects the whole

Different emotional blocks manifest in a different combination of organs, but it is not necessary to know these; it is enough to know that the part affects the whole. So if we treat the whole, the part will be healed. No part can be seen in isolation as it also causes a disruption to the flow of all other parts.

The body messages are like a hologram. Each cell has complete knowledge of the other cells. The body is a great communicating system within itself. It is an intelligent system, so cutting out the affected area does not take away the original conflict as it is still contained within all that remains.

It is a common complaint that the Western conventional medical way sees each part in isolation. We see an eye specialist for eye problems, a back specialist for back complaints, a kidney specialist for a kidney disease and a psychiatrist for our mind. Many doctors are now integrating 'spirit' with science and are beginning to realise that the mental and emotional state of a patient is the key to successful treatment. Doctors increasingly refer their patients to learn Reiki, join a gym, receive massage, aromatherapy, reflexology, counselling and other healers. I have taught many doctors, nurses and others in the caring professions who find Reiki has the added bonus of self-treatment for their own well-being.

If we do not address the cause, the body will inevitably re-create the conflict of energy in some other part of us. We must take heed, not only the moment our bodies begin to complain but also at all other times, to assist our energy in transforming what is being absorbed.

Life is a journey

Life is a journey, a place of learning. The most important lesson is to reconnect with the source of our being in order to surf the waves instead of swim or drown.

How do we do that? We may not like to admit we are lost because then we have to begin the seemingly endless search to be found. The illusion is that we think we are lost when, in fact, we never went anywhere; we were always, in essence, found.

First, we look for the answer in relationships, in power over others, in the accumulation of wealth or the struggle to obtain wealth, in a fine car, in alcohol, drugs, sex. For a time pleasure is gained from all the above but they become addictions as the material pleasure is an illusion and therefore temporary. We expected so much and were only disappointed. We could define an expectation as a disappointment about to happen. We should have known.

When, finally, we awaken to realise how lost we are, we may even cry out from our despair 'please help me', then we are on the way to being found. You cannot be found unless first you recognise that you are lost.

Perhaps you sought out this book because you have a physical disease, or maybe mental, emotional, relationship difficulties.

Whatever the reason a method is needed to help you rediscover your true self, a method that is simple, one you can understand and practise in your daily life. Self-discovery is an incredible and surprising process. New worlds open up to you. 'Ask and it shall be given unto you', 'Seek ye first the Kingdom of Heaven that is within' and know that the state of Heaven on Earth is achievable for you. Know you are worthy of it and it will become yours.

Have you ever asked yourself 'What is my purpose on this Earth?' and 'Why am I suffering?' You can make up a good reason, a philosophy even, but do you *know*?

We all want to love and be loved, but at the same time, we feel somewhat separated and isolated from others, we feel insecure as everything we hold on to changes. That, unfortunately, is a fundamental law of nature, 'everything that can change will change'. We have to touch the unchanging, the constant part of us, the place that never changes.

Self-examination

Self-examination can be scary, as we may have grown to dislike ourselves or even fear looking within as we have suffered so much at the hands of others. In your deepest despair you called out, and nobody came. Did you not realise then that only *you* can heal yourself? We need a way out of being at the mercy of others, we need to wake up to what is right for us at this time, for that is all we can ever know. We can no longer live other people's expectations of us if we are once more to become ourselves.

The reason no one ever told you this is that they, too, were lost and had no answer – the blind leading the blind. We must learn to integrate a method to help us know our Divine Nature and regain well-being. We need something simple, uncomplicated, easy to understand, tangible, for the phrase 'to be able to see the unseen' is very confusing. Touch the 'unseen' with your hands, find where it resides and what it can do, after all it is the energy that created us in the beginning and keeps re-creating us at every moment.

7

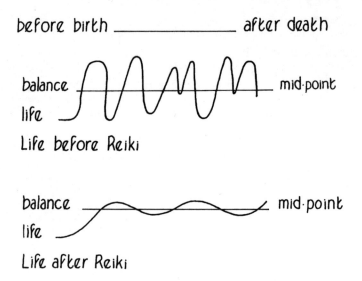

before birth ———————————— after death

balance

life

Life before Reiki

balance

life

Life after Reiki

Self-knowledge

Self-knowledge is a breaking away from the Tribal Mind – that is, the negative group mentality that tells us the answer lies in a bigger car, a more beautiful wife, a jam doughnut. It is a stepping back from the destructive influence of the world. When we look within we do it because we know there is a possibility that we may find, otherwise why bother? When we allow more energy to flow into us our bodies are regenerated, our minds settle to become less confused, our emotions become clear. Our soul comes Home. We become integrated instead of disintegrated; a constitutional change takes place; every cell of the body awakens, the physiology changes, the chemistry is different. Just think of the difference between being depressed, when the body is heavy to drag along, the mind is in a negative fog and nothing works, to being in love when everything sparkles, the body floats along, the energy is upwards, you don't even need much sleep and you can conquer the world. The chemistry can be measured and it will be very different.

FIND THE SOURCE

So to fill the body with love and light we must find the source of that light. Reiki is a method to reconnect with the source, to learn in a practical way to access the energy with your hands and replenish yourself. Reiki is not the *only* way to re-awaken ourselves for there are indeed many ways, but it is a very good starting point.

That which you are looking for is inside of you.

Maharaji

LISTENING HANDS EXERCISE – CONTEMPLATION

Contemplation is not merely thinking about something logically and rationally, it is to observe a quality within a phrase or thought and let go, allowing the quality to sink into the subconscious and become a part of your feeling self. It is not how you think but how you know. At the end of each chapter you will find a phrase to contemplate. Take each one by itself for a day and be serious about it. Sit quietly with it, think about it, even discuss it. Each has the potential for deep transformation.

ORIGINS OF
THE FORM

No man can reveal to you aught but that which already is half asleep in the dawning of your knowledge.

Khalil Gilbran, *The Prophet*

DR USUI DISCOVERS REIKI

Dr Mikao Usui

At the end of the nineteenth century there lived a man called Dr Mikao Usui in a monastery in Kyoto, Japan. It is said that he was a Christian professor of Theology at Doshina University. At the time of the graduation of his students Dr Usui was asked the question 'How, exactly, did Jesus heal?' He could not give a clear answer as he, too, had lived on belief and trust in the truth of Bible stories. He resigned his post at the college and went in search of an answer.

He studied many other scriptures apart from Christian texts. He travelled to America and spent seven years in Chicago where he received a Doctorate in Scripture at the university. He eventually returned to Japan where he learnt the ancient language of Sanskrit, with its origins in India, and began reading scriptures that describe Japanese Buddhism. He spent much time with monks in a Buddhist monastery reading these ancient texts and learning the sutras and mantras. One day he happened upon something that greatly excited him. There in the scriptures was a passage on healing which contained a formula written in symbolic form.

Meditation on the Holy Mountain

The monks explained that their focus was on the spiritual aspect of healing through Buddhism, rather than the healing of the mind and body, therefore the symbols were no longer understood by them.

Dr Usui knew the symbols held the answer to what he was looking for. They were the keys to the healing ways of the Buddha, Christ and other spiritual leaders yet there were no instructions. He recognised the symbols as being sacred and special. In order to understand them better he decided to use his experience of deep meditation to learn the essence from within himself as triggered by each symbol.

Symbols are powerful tools, they are keys to unlock and access our other levels of consciousness. They contain within their simple structure the whole content of their form and the process which they activate. (Symbols will be explained in further detail in Chapter 6.) Dr Usui understood the symbols to be the keys to healing he had been searching for, but their content was not made clear, so he took them into deep meditation on a nearby holy mountain, Mount Kuriyama. He sat by a stream with no food and placed before him twenty-one stones to count the days. He told the monks that in twenty-one days either he would have found the answer or they could collect his dead body.

The twenty-first day dawned and as he threw away the last stone a light came rushing towards him knocking him into another state of consciousness. In his mind's eye, as if on a screen, he saw each symbol in a golden bubble of light. He held on to each image until an understanding washed through him. When all the symbols had passed through in this way, they had burned themselves into his memory.

Awakening to something special

Dr Usui arose changed in some way. He came down the mountain feeling surprisingly well and strong. However, he tripped on a rock stubbing his toe. His immediate reaction was to put his hands there. He noticed how quickly the pain subsided and the bleeding stopped. He had begun the task of gathering evidence that something had taken place.

As he continued his descent of the mountain he stopped at a stall selling breakfast. The vendor, realising that Dr Usui had been fasting, told him to rest and wait for the preparation of a special light meal for his delicate and empty stomach. Dr Usui rested under a tree. The meal was brought out by the young daughter of the vendor who was obviously in much pain due to a swollen tooth abscess. Dr Usui asked if he could place his hands gently on her face and as he did so the pain subsided, the swelling disappeared. Dr Usui realised that truly something special had happened to him.

Healing the sick

Dr Usui spent the next seven years living in the beggars' quarters of Kyoto, healing and teaching, but realised that, in spite of their new-found health, the beggars quickly returned to their old ways. When he asked them why they had not moved on they replied 'This is who we are, what we were born to be, it is all we know'. Dr Usui was sad but understood that healing the physical problem is not enough.

A corresponding mental, spiritual attitude is needed also. So he began to teach the Five Precepts of Reiki.

The Five Precepts of Reiki

- Just for today do not anger
- Just for today do not worry
- Earn your living honestly
- Honour your parents, elders and teachers
- Give gratitude to every living thing and every situation.

Dr Hayashi

Dr Chujiro Hayashi

Dr Usui saw the need to look for people who would honour his teaching as precious but also have the desire for change. He met a remarkable man, Dr Chujiro Hayashi, who was a retired naval officer and an aristocrat. Dr Hayashi was keen to assist in healing, having witnessed the destruction of war at first hand. He was initiated into Reiki and set up a clinic in Tokyo called *Shina No Machi*.

When Dr Usui's life was drawing to an end he recognised Hayashi as the Master of Reiki and charged him with keeping the essence of his teachings pure and intact and in their original form. Hayashi agreed to this and made extensive records to demonstrate that Reiki finds the source of physical symptoms, fills the being with vitality and restores the person into wholeness.

Hawayo Takata meets Dr Hayashi

Hawayo Takata

In 1935 a lady called Hawayo Takata came to Dr Hayashi's clinic having been diagnosed with many ills including a tumour for which she was about to undergo an operation. Takata had lived in Hawaii until, in her mid-twenties, her husband suddenly died leaving her grief stricken and alone with two small children. The grief created such illness in her that a tumour formed. However, when she returned to Japan for an operation a voice inside her said 'There is another way'. She was directed to Dr Hayashi's clinic where she was treated every day for eight months by which time she had fully recovered. She became a dedicated student working in the clinic, but not learning Reiki as women were not allowed to become Masters.

Over the years she showed a deep commitment to Reiki and eventually Hayashi broke with tradition and initiated her into First Degree.

The Master Line expands

During the Second World War Hayashi was called up to fight the Americans. Being a Reserve naval officer his first duty was to his country and therefore to fight. Being a Universal Healer his duty was also to heal all beings and see them as one. His dilemma was so great that he gathered together all his family and colleagues for a meeting. At the meeting he declared Takata would carry on the lineage and teach Reiki as a Master keeping the original form and essence pure and simple. He then said 'There is no such thing as death only great change' and left his body. His body fell back; he had gone into transition. The mark of enlightenment and lack of stress showed in the fact that his body did not decay as a normal body would. It remained unchanged for many weeks. (This also happened to the great sage Paramahansa Yogananda.)

Takata's twenty-two Masters

Takata took Reiki back to Hawaii and introduced her gift to the Western world. She died in 1980 having trained twenty-two Reiki Masters.

The twenty-two Masters created by Takata are:

- Wanja Twan
- Barbara Ray
- Mary McFadden
- Fran Brown
- Iris Ishikuro
- Virginia Samdahl

- Shimobu Saito (Takata's sister)
- Phyllis Lei Furumoto (Takata's grand-daughter)
- Paul Mitchell
- Seiji Takimori
- Bethel Phaigh
- Barbara McCullogh
- George Arak
- Dorothy Baba
- Ursula Baylow
- Rick Bockner
- Barbara Brown
- Patricia Ewing
- Beth Gray
- John Gray
- Harry Kubai
- Ethel Lombardi

Wanja Twan's story

Wanja Twan

Wanja Twan is Swedish and lives in British Columbia, Canada. She is a weaver and potter. One morning her husband said 'I'm off now' and left – for good, leaving Wanja with a farm and six children to look after. She was, therefore, very stressed by the prospect but being a Devotee of Guru Muktanand she had great trust in the Divine Gift. She put out to her teacher to take care of her. Soon she heard of a Japanese lady (Takata) who had come to the area to teach people healing. Wanja met Takata and a deep friendship was born. Wanja was initiated and later became a Master. She has taught Reiki to many of the native Indians and helped them to regain their confidence in their heritage and self-worth. She, in return, has been privileged to learn Shamanism from them – American Indian healing through altered states, knowledge of non-ordinary reality and earth remedies.

A meeting of Masters in India

In the early 1980s Wanja went on a visit to India to see her Guru, Muktanand. There she was introduced to another devotee called Martha Sylvester. Martha was staying in the same Ashram and had heard of Reiki but put aside the thought of learning about it until she returned to England. She was surprised one day when her room mate told her 'You'll never believe it, there's a Reiki Master in the Ashram'. Martha was later initiated and eventually became a Master herself in 1985.

My meeting with Wanja

I came to Reiki through my T'ai Chi teacher who offered it as a way to assist our growth and understanding of ourselves. I met Martha Sylvester in 1988 and received First Degree. I also received Second Degree in 1988 and began working with Martha organising her classes and assisting her. Martha was, then, one of only about five or six Masters in this country; there are now several hundred.

Sandi Leir Shuffrey

In 1989 I was privileged to meet Wanja Twan when she came to Cardiff to see Martha. I arrived late, which is unlike me, to find only one chair left – in front of Wanja. It was my fortune. Wanja gazed into me with her penetrating blue eyes and thereafter instructed Martha to make me a Master.

I became a Master in 1989, an offer that comes only once in a lifetime. For this I undertook two years of apprenticeship, was initiated when six months' pregnant and taught my first class when nine months' pregnant. Martha taught me well, she left me on my own and said 'Let the Reiki do the talking'. She was right. Another phrase she often repeated was 'You only get what you can handle with Reiki'. This is how Reiki can take you way beyond the limitations and expectations of yourself. In nine years I have taught only two further teaching Masters who each trained with me for more than six years. Reiki chooses its own Masters. Takata did not teach anyone else for over thirty-seven years.

Being initiated as a Master is only the beginning of the commitment. True Mastery comes about through humility.

How long do we have to work on ourselves? – Always and forever.

'Wisdom'

LISTENING HANDS EXERCISE – RE-LAX BREATH MEDITATION

Find a quiet room and a comfortable chair where you will not be disturbed for twenty minutes by the telephone, the children or the cat. Dim the lights or draw the curtains. Decide to put your worries aside for now. Without effort, notice that you are breathing – one breath in and one breath out. That is how it happens. When a breath comes in allow your mind to say the sound 'Re' as in relax, and as the breath goes out allow the mind to say 'Lax'. Do not force the breath and do not breathe to the word, rather say the word to the breath. An in-breath 'Re' creates a state of anticipation in the body, the out-breath 'Lax' allows all tensions to let go. After ten to fifteen minutes notice how you feel. How is the body? How is the mind? Is there a little more stillness, a little more silence?

3

WHAT IS REIKI?

Always aim for the highest as achievable, for if you only aim for the next step, only the next step will become yours.

Maharishi

How does Reiki work?

The Dharma Wheel – Symbol of the Laws of the Universe. The threefold spiral that is perfect balance, positive, negative and neutral, or equilibrium.

Reiki is simple, it is practical, it is a technique for healing, yet it is more than just a technique it is a way of being, the by-product of which is wholeness and harmony. It is an activator, releaser and transformer of subtle energies. It is the power of Love.

The body's natural leaning is towards balance as it is an intelligent sensory organ. Our minds and emotions hold the body out of order, often through simple ignorance, because the way we are is how we have been conditioned by others to think and feel. As you think, so it shall become. If, for a moment, we put our personality aside then our body knows how to be well. Its intuitive self will draw in anything nearby that can replenish it or lead it to whatever herb or person it needs at that time to be well.

Reiki is a natural balancing energy. It is not positive life force, it is balance. It is therefore positive, negative and neutral for only then can it manifest. The Law of Manifestation says: *Everything manifests out of the infinite ocean of non-existence and de-manifests there once again.* Reiki cleanses the body and quietens the mind. Quieten the mind and the body relaxes – releases. Release from the body and the mind will quieten. The result of a cleansed body is a cleared mind. If the mind is agitated there is usually a corresponding tension, stress or pain held in the body. So being held in stillness and silence with an access to healing energy gives the whole self a window of opportunity for restoration. The heart then opens and the spirit can be experienced. When firmly established as an experience and a familiar feeling, the spirit can begin to manifest a reorganisation of the body to become more constructive, dynamic, effective and free from illness.

Three avenues of nourishment

The three main avenues through which the body draws in energy from outside are:

- Food/water
- Prana/breath
- Subtle body senses – Universal Energy/Reiki

The senses of hearing, sight, smell, taste and, to some extent, touch are for experiencing an understanding of the outside world, which really only mirrors our internal world.

The three avenues are used in combination. Unfortunately, in our modern polluted world there are also avenues of destruction, poison and imbalance. So the body needs assistance to access the subtle energies directly. Much of our food is devoid of life force by being frozen, dried and refined. Our air is full of unseen chemicals, we are fed fear by the media which gradually subsumes us. Excess fear produces a state of adrenaline 'poisoning' which is hard to dissipate.

Change to be well

Food

Change to a lighter, fresher, more varied diet that contains life force. Eat fewer dairy products, which are binding and mucous forming and may contain hormones or antibiotic traces to which many of us are allergic, more fruit and vegetables and less meat. Drink more water, to bring back the homeostasis and create a healthy 'electrical' circuit. Drink less tea, coffee, alcohol and carbonised drinks. These are either stimulants or depressants and cause ups and downs. Our food and drink causes changes in our blood quality and nervous reactions. We also need rest and sleep. Listen to your body.

Prana

Breathe. We breathe in that which has been breathed out by other plants and animals, therefore we are interrelated. Breathe deeply but naturally and gently. In fact, let the breath breathe you. Shallow or rapid breathing causes mental agitation – likewise mental agitation causes shallow or rapid breathing. During periods of stress or depression it is even possible to hardly breathe at all, starving the body of oxygen and vitality. An imbalance in the gas levels in the brain creates imbalance in the thought processes, reactions and ability to cope with stress, toxins, etc. The purpose of breath is to draw in oxygen and expel carbon dioxide – draw in life force and expel that which is no longer needed.

Exercise in fresh air is the quickest way to remedy oxygen depletion. Exercise itself helps free toxins which may then be eliminated more rapidly as the metabolism speeds up.

SUBTLE BODY

External Energram Field interacting with the environment

Einstein proved that light and matter are interchangeable. Reiki is light from which matter is re-created. Light is the first manifestation of being. Reiki is the subtle energy that replenishes the subtle body. It is drawn through you yet not from you; it is not your own energy that is passed through but that from the unlimited reservoir. It is drawn into the receiving body to wherever it is needed. The body being intelligent is also aware of where the energy is needed, which may be different from where the pain is felt. In giving Reiki you are also receiving as it is drawn through. In this way it is your protection from absorbing the pain or stresses of the person receiving. You should not feel tired and drained after giving Reiki but relaxed and energised.

The Reiki energy flashes through the body to the cellular level enlivening and awakening each cell with light. The cells as they are stimulated in turn release their own tensions and toxins; they signal to one another and gradually the whole system lightens up. This is the true meaning of enlightenment. The corresponding reaction in the mind is clarity. Our tensions flow into the bloodstream and are dispelled through the eliminatory organs.

As blocked emotions and traumas are stored in the cells they too become free and may even disappear without the need for years of therapy. A great feeling of freedom may occur. In this way the past may be healed in the present, thereby creating a different future.

TREATING THE WHOLE BY TREATING THE PART

A Reiki treatment covers the whole body, focusing on individual areas and major organs, but it can be received by just holding the hand or foot. Often when people are seriously ill a whole body treatment is inappropriate. Holding the hand of someone dying is a great comfort and allows them to draw in unconditional love without words.

The form of Reiki therapy as a whole body treatment is described in Chapter 5.

a cleansing period

There is a common theory that it takes twenty-one days to fully cleanse the system. I disagree, for if each individual is unique, has a unique set of circumstances, blocks, conflicts, etc. and a unique way of dealing with them, then each treatment, even on the same person, creates a unique cleansing that may be instant or infinite. Cleansing is an ongoing process. Like life, it is a peeling away of layers to reveal other layers. It is true that purification may feel uncomfortable but there can be no time limit put on it as energy in transformation is not in the realm of time.

Environmental osmosis and constitution

Our subtle bodies are constantly being influenced by the environment as well as by our personality, the atmosphere, weather, climate, seasons, months, hours. Even the aspects of the planets at the moment we are born influence our individuality, and the Moon has a hold over our emotions.

We form our inner environment, our constitution, from the air, water, minerals, plant and animal life that we ingest together with their corresponding electromagnetic vibrations. The balance between our external and internal environment creates our physical and mental planes; it is an interaction, a participation with our environment. The external has infinite dimension while the internal is limited by our physical boundaries: it is more dense and compact yet also subject to change. The incoming and outgoing energy must balance or there will be overexpansion or degeneration. Our basic constitution is created by our inherited genetic patterning and by our mother's diet before we are born, also her physical and mental attitude during gestation. Constitutional change is slow, expanding and contracting like a breath, while the external conditions change rapidly, being influenced by all other things that are in motion.

A shift of awareness

Reiki is all-powerful and, therefore, can influence the constitution. It can repattern our genetic traits, through release of present constrictions, to align with a more Divine and conscious evolution.

Having a perfect and well body is not the answer; we are looking for a change in attitude. Just a simple shift in awareness will change a person's whole life and thereby their constitution. When Reiki is applied in a practical sense the whole system is revitalised. I teach my students to expect nothing more than a subtle shift of awareness. If they expect miracles, miracles can't happen. So I set them up to expect nothing and they are astounded at the magic in their hands.

We tend to see illness as a weakness that has 'come to get us' rather than a starting point in a journey in which we can realise our potential, inner strength and wisdom.

We are all light in motion.

LISTENING hANDS EXERCISE – LISTENING WITh ThE hANDS

Sit in your quiet place undisturbed for twenty minutes, palms up on your lap. Begin with five minutes of Re-lax breath. Then allow the attention to move down into the upturned palms. Notice what sensations are there. Tingling? Heat? Cold? Swirling? Nothing? Notice the difference on the in-breath to the out-breath. Notice the difference at the point of change where in turns to out and out turns to in. Can you feel the waves turn in your hands? Can you feel the magnetism? Can you feel the potential for transference of this energy?

4

THE PRINCIPLES THAT GOVERN THE ORIGINAL FORM

Intention shapes the light of your consciousness
which in turn creates your reality.

Students of Reiki learn a practical technique for hands-on healing that is useful in everyday life. This technique is taught to bring about physical, emotional, mental and spiritual well-being for self and others. The technique is not the Form, it is a part of it. Many people today *do the course* in order to *become healers*. No one can heal anyone except themselves. They are merely assistants/ facilitators to others. Awareness of the levels of the Form must be taught and understood.

PERSONAL GROWTH

This is an awakening of the senses to the environment and the Divine content therein, a conscious change, a choice to learn and grow, for choice not chance fashions our destiny. Self-treatment brings about self-awareness. It alters the stressed state and we become more able to yield in the face of adversity. Pain is often our route to freedom; it contains a solution.

There are no short cuts to personal growth, two steps forwards, one step back, so it seems. Even when we feel nothing is happening everything is still moving forwards.

Spiritual Discipline

This is an awakening to the Spirit as Being and its interconnectedness with all forms, a purification, a falling away of the masks that cause an illusion of suffering. An awareness of our own Sacredness becomes apparent. There is no turning back once the path is undertaken. Once you know you can never un-know.

Experience through practice achieves this level of awareness, yet it is not always at first understood. The attitude of patience is gained through trust of the whole Form. The initiation makes direct contact with our spirit and is made tangible through giving to others and self-treatment. The relationship with oneself improves to a quality of self-love.

Mystic Order

This is a community of people who commonly recognise the Mystery of the Universal Energy in action. People who have received the Reiki initiation naturally are a part of this. The mystic order, however, is not mysterious. Reiki is our essential nature from which we have become separated and hidden ourselves with masks of anger, jealousy, greed and ignorance, etc. If God were truly a mystery or a strange vision then it would not be possible for the experience to be revealed to us. There is no belief system within Reiki but there is a common experience of the gift of life itself. One breath in, one breath out, that is no mystery. It is all we are. When we know, we may sit quietly in humility, inspiring and leading others also to the Mastery of their Soul.

Initiation

Initiation is a sacred ritual that creates a focus of attention. It is a turning point, a new way, a beginning. The student agrees to receive

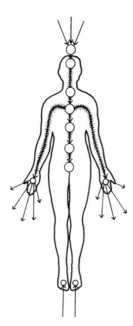

The Reiki pathway through the energy centres (chakras)

and gives a gift of exchange to create the gateway that will be received. The body has seven major centres of concentrated energy that are called *chakras*. These are located on the crown of the head, the brow, the throat, the heart, the solar plexus, the navel and the reproductive organs. These natural healing centres of the body already exist and are neither opened nor closed but realigned in such a way that the energy access is made available and does not revert to its original form. The initiations are the essential part of the Form, the difference between Reiki and all other forms of healing. They allow the path of energy to be drawn down through the top of the head, through the heart, into the solar plexus and out through the hands. They alter the vibrational flow of the body and align it in such a way as to gain permanent access to the source of all things. I use the analogy of a hose-pipe turned on but with a kink in it. The Master has been trained to find the kink and undo it so the water can flow freely once again. It is really nothing new, only a remembering.

There are four initiations for First Degree, one for Second Degree and one for Master's Degree. Each is performed individually in silence by a fully trained Master who does not interfere with the process through their ego and realises the serious nature of this moment for the student. It brings about a union with the Reiki. It is a ritual of invocation and direction of the Light, a holy act of purification. The initiation in itself will transform as it changes the essential vibrational frequency of the student. The frequency with which the soul-self of the student operates is raised so that what is put out is in balance and harmony, therefore what comes back in circumstance and relationship is also in balance and harmony.

ORAL TRADITION

This is the energetic transference by word of mouth and by personal instruction in the presence and under the guidance of a Reiki Master directly and individually to the student.

The class Form is the completion of the tradition i.e. initiation, exchange, history, understanding, positions, questions and answers, inspiration. Oral tradition has currently been diluted by well-meaning New Age people who have 'channelled' from the dead Masters new symbols and instructions. If the Form had not been complete in its simplicity then I doubt that Dr Usui would have passed it on as such.

HISTORICAL LINEAGE

This is the line of Masters who have orally transmitted their knowledge to their chosen apprentices and students. The history is a description or myth of events in the past that link us to the present and inspire us to see other's lives and paths as symbolic to our own. It is an essential part of the oral tradition to know our roots and respect the original principles.

Spiritual Lineage

Not necessarily the Historic Line, spiritual lineage is said to be held by Phyllis Furomoto, as agreed by the Reiki Alliance of Masters based in America. There are many other lineage bearers in the world, especially those students in Japan whose history is direct from Usui or Hayashi without any connection to Takata. The Lineage Bearer embodies the essence of the system and with great conscience maintains its purity, simplicity, and upholds to inspire others to their own integrity, as indeed I do. It is my understanding, however, that anyone who upholds the purity, the sacred tradition and the element of simplicity also bears the Spirit Line, as there is neither hierarchy nor individual focus in the realm of Universal Energy. Exclusivity of any part must mean deviation from the truth. I honour my vows and endeavour to uphold the precepts.

The Spiritual Precepts

- Just for today do not anger ... Just for today I am at peace.
- Just for today do not worry ... Just for today my mind is at rest.
- Honour your parents, elders, teachers ... I honour my parents, elders, teachers, children and friends.
- Earn your living honestly ... I earn my living honestly and do no harm to anyone, anything or the environment.
- Give gratitude to every living thing ... I give thanks to every living thing and every situation whatever form it may take for within it is contained my growth and understanding.

Exchange

Money is an energy system. It is a paper symbol of an agreed quantity, a value, an exchange for gold. We constantly exchange this energy for others: petrol, gas, electricity, food, clothes, time, labour, etc. Each level of Reiki has an appropriate amount of exchange which is enough to make people think about their level of commitment to it.

- First Degree should be around two day's average wage.
- Second Degree should be around one week's average wage.
- Master's Degree is by invitation only and is around six or seven months' average wage for training and apprenticeship. This level is a lifetime's commitment.

Masters Degree initiation without teaching level is available for about two weeks' average wage. This is for those wishing for the shift in energy level and understanding without the apprenticeship and commitment necessary to teach.

To pay 'bucket-shop' prices for this empowerment is to receive a diamond for the price of spinach, or rather, receiving spinach as you paid the price of spinach when what you really wanted was the diamond. You get what you pay for.

In America, Australia and some New Age centres in Britain it is possible to do all three degrees in three days. This is like giving a monkey a chain-saw to do the pruning just because it can climb trees. Proper, careful training is necessary with a long-enough break in between to assimilate the knowledge.

When money is exchanged there is an energetic transference. Many people think that by giving healing for free and teaching Reiki on the cheap they are doing humanity a service. They are, however, assisting people in being limited. The exchange does not have to be money. I have a rose arch, a painted hallway, kitchen unit doors, etc. all provided by exchange. Each act was done with respect for the principle and an understanding of the sacredness of the gift that had been received.

The Master's level can be learnt in New Age centres for as little as one week's average wage in one weekend, after only practising First and Second Degree for a matter of days or of weeks. Would you trust your car maintenance to someone who had only ever seen a pushbike? I don't think so. This is your life and happiness we are talking about.

Generally, a training Master must have practised Reiki for at least three years before beginning apprenticeship; this may in itself last two or three years. Permission must be gained from the initiating Master's own master and preferably a meeting arranged between the three.

Once the Master is initiated he or she is still an apprentice, gradually paying off the guidance fee. Once the exchange is complete the

Master feels ready to hatch out of the protection of the Master to become the Mastery. Every class and every person brings about a new learning for the new Master. No training is ever complete. Reiki chooses its own Masters yet the current Master looks for certain signs in candidates. Their true conscience tells who is the right person and what is the right time. It is not a personal choice, it is the only choice.

There is a tradition of exchange in the history of Reiki but this is money only when in the realm of a professional Reiki therapist. Otherwise, with friends and family just the awareness of the gift with an exchange of an errand run, a bunch of flowers from the garden or assistance in some other way is all that is necessary. When I first treated my parents, and subsequently taught them, the exchange they made was to lie down and receive, for parents can be constant givers and not be able to receive. In receiving you are allowing the other person to have the pleasure of giving.

We pay our homoeopath, acupuncturist, chiropractor, a set fee. Reiki practitioners also give their time and dedication to the client. They have to pay the bills and feed their children. If healing is for free then the client frequently does not participate in their process of well-being, often leaving it up to the healer to heal. This is not taking responsibility but passing it on to someone else, reinforcing their own weakness. They must realise that the practitioner is only the access for their own self to heal itself. No personal credit is taken for the effects of Reiki – it does itself.

Symbols

There are three symbols for Second Degree and one for Master's Degree. These are used at initiation. They are described more fully in the section on Second Degree Class Form.

Treatment

A whole body treatment takes between an hour and an hour and a half. It uses contact and connection through the hands in a set sequence that is flexible and adaptable according to the circumstances. People

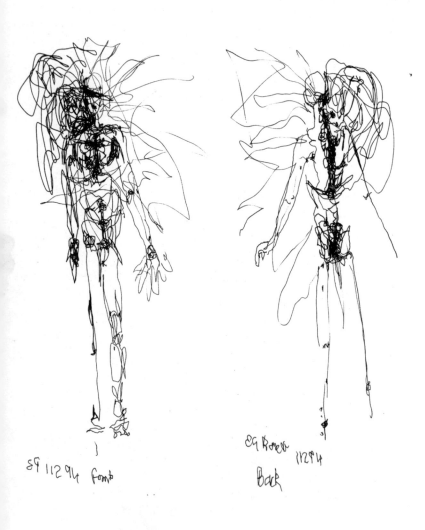

The Internal Energram Field showing energy blocks

who cannot lie down may sit up. The formula is a good guideline to follow. It has been worked out carefully to flow through the whole body without bringing the receiver back from their deep relaxation by the interruption of the hands moving. This is the grounding or earthing of the spiritual aspects of the Form. The Being into Becoming. Holding the person in stillness and silence to see that part of themselves that is usually masked by sight, sound and the distraction of worldly activity. A scary place? No, a beautiful place. The giver observes the experiences of the receiver with interest and sometimes with awe and wonder as magic seems to occur, always giving gratitude to the force itself at the end and taking no credit.

The First and Second Degree classes are aimed at people who want to practise first on themselves and second on friends and family, to improve their own set of illnesses, relationships and circumstances.

Never leave room for doubt in your mind.

Maharaji

LISTENING HANDS EXERCISE – ENERGY SENSING

Stand in the garden barefoot, facing east, feet shoulder-width apart, knees unlocked or slightly bent, tail tucked in, shoulders relaxed, arms by the side, eyes closed. On an in-breath slowly raise the arms to the side, hands softly relaxed, and up to the head in a gentle round circle, keeping arms in front of the shoulders to avoid any tension. On an out-breath allow the arms to circle down. Take a whole breath in to reach the top and a whole breath out to reach the bottom, then repeat. Notice how the breath slows down after four to five minutes. Stand relaxed and notice the sensation in the body, in the palms, in the head and in the feet. Wait a few minutes and repeat twice more.

5 REIKI IN PRACTICE – The LISTENING hANDS TECHNIQUE

If we still and expand the mind, its reflection,
which is the visible world, expands with it.

The FORM OF The CLASS

The class must support the aspect of purity and simplicity first and foremost with nothing added from other disciplines: no New Age music, no gongs or chants, *no clearing of stuff*. It must contain only Reiki if students are to know what they are receiving. It must not be diluted with other ideas or dogmas, crystals, rattles or drums. These have a sacred place also but they are not appropriate here. It is for the Master, the Reiki and the student alone, for the student can experience what Reiki is only when they quieten the clutter of the mind and look within.

Reiki classes are a unique way of learning. Most other classes are taught with the aid of notebooks and pens. Much structure and information is given out to re-read at a later date and remind yourself not to forget. Reiki is not learnt with the mind, it is a full experience and therefore cannot be forgotten. The initiations implant the connection within you, like putting up a radio aerial and tuning it into a particular frequency.

FOUR SESSIONS

The class is usually set out in four sessions, with one initiation at the beginning of each session to allow the alignment to be gradual, and a practical grounding session in between. In my classes I begin by introducing myself, how I came to Reiki and what it has done for me. I then form an energetic group by allowing people to introduce themselves and why they are here. The history of Reiki is then told, followed by the meaning of Reiki and how it works. I allow a long question-and-answer session to make sure people are clear. I explain the principles as set out in Chapter 4.

Generally, anyone who is more than twelve weeks' pregnant will be asked to return in about a year as, once the foetus is fully formed, it is felt that it is being initiated also but without personal permission. It is, however, totally safe to learn, give and receive Reiki during pregnancy. It has great benefits to the pregnant mother, relieving side effects such as nausea, backache, etc. and is wonderful during labour to replenish between contractions and prevent trauma.

I ask people to inform me in private in the initiating room of their medication and especially if they are undergoing, or have undergone in the past, treatment for depression or mental illness or suffer from any phobia or eating disorder. Reiki sensitises some people and care must be taken of them. Students may not dare to come to learn if they feel they have to participate in a group lunch. It may be inappropriate to teach some people but refer them to treatment instead.

During the introduction of the group it is possible, when experienced, to detect those people who do not want to fully *become part of a group*. An eye must be kept on these people to assist them to overcome whatever hurdle their fears have placed in front of them which may prevent them completing the course. Of course, if someone wishes to leave that wish must be respected. I give everyone the opportunity to leave before the commitment of exchange and initiation.

It is important to note that Reiki cannot be used for negative intent such as black magic or power over others as it always brings light and balance into being. Darkness cannot be empowered by light.

INITIATION

The energy exchange is made as people prepare to enter the first initiation. Once initiated, the energy begins to come through. A demonstration is given of the first series of positions on the head and heart. It is stressed that the head and heart positions are the most important but a whole body treatment is most beneficial to finding the root cause. It is not necessary to remove any clothing except shoes and spectacles. The treatment is a personal internal act and this aspect must be respected at all times, therefore no intimate positions are to be included and no invasion of privacy.

A Listening Hands exercise is given to allow the sense of touch to be looked into. The lightness with which we place our hands on another is very important. We must not lean in by being heavy handed nor by hovering and being hesitant. The exercise brings the listening skill of our intuitive self out from our ears and into our hands.

Awareness is focused on the interface between our hands and the body receiving which is where any changes are felt. A practitioner may have very cold physical hands but the person receiving experiences burning heat; what they feel is not body temperature but the transference of energy as it is drawn through.

Practise couches are used in class but may not always be available. At home we have to adapt by using a sofa or a bed. When the practice sessions begin, each student is personally guided and observed by the Master who must remain in the room. Every person covers every position and receives the experience for themselves from another person. Often we work in groups of three with the third person holding the feet.

FIRST SESSION – HEAD AND HEART POSITIONS

There is no need to take down a lengthy case history involving friends and family, nor even to delve into people's problems. It is necessary only to ask if there are any structural problems i.e. back injury, to avoid any injury or strain as the receiver is helped on to a bed or couch. Lying down is the best position, but for some people sitting in a chair will suffice. All the positions can be adapted accordingly.

The treatment begins with preparation of the giver and a gentle introduction of the two bodies by a non-invasive, gentle stroke to the forehead. Each position is held for between three and five minutes to allow the energy to dissolve stress in that area to trigger a drawing-in process.

During a class each position is carefully instructed, observed and explained in detail along with its physical and emotional content.

Position 1

The first position is with the hands placed gently over the eyes. This takes the sense of sight inwards, quietening the mind and allowing the energy to be drawn in to all parts of the head and even through to the far reaches of the body. It slows down the outward projection of the soul allowing stillness and inward exploration to begin. This relates to the Brow Chakra, the colour of which is purple or violet.

Position 2

The second position is over the top of the head, either side of the brain, to balance the brain and quieten the mind. It is especially beneficial for combating stress, remembering and learning difficulties. This relates to the Crown Chakra, the colour of which is white or sometimes gold.

Position 3

The third position is around the jaw. The muscles here are strong and hold on tight to unexpressed anger. This feels soothing, like being 'held in the mother's arms.'

Position 4

The fourth position is with the hands cupped under the back of the head. This is a very supportive position, particularly effective for combating exhaustion, anxiety, headache and mental tension. For severe headache or migraine I place one hand under the head and one over the forehead so the relaxation can be generated from both sides. This relates to the Alter Major Chakra, the colour of which is brown. This centre is in addition to the seven rainbow colours on the front of the body.

Position 5

The fifth position is a simple cupping of the ears. Reiki has been found to reduce tinnitus and even repair the nerve damage that causes deafness. It is a great pain reliever for children's ear infections. This position takes the sense of hearing inwards to enhance the inner awareness and lessen the outward projection to which we are addicted. Many people relax by listening to a distraction, the television, radio or music, missing out on the profound experience of stillness and silence. It is said, by the sages, that the initiation into the Inner Sound Current is the highest vehicle for enlightenment.

Position 6

The sixth position is over the throat. The throat is the area of communication, how we express ourselves. It is often noted that the voice becomes clearer and deeper. This relates to the Throat Chakra, the colour of which is blue.

Position 7

The heart. The seat of unconditional love and emotion. This position also governs the immune system. Many of our illnesses are produced from a lack of a trusting heart caused by negative past experiences. The hands on the heart allow it to warm, soften and open which, in time, creates the ability to stand and face the world 'square on'. If our emotions hold us down, then to heal this area can lift us up. This relates to the Heart Chakra, the colour of which is green.

Position 8

The hands hold the soft part of the shoulder towards the underarm. This allows energy to pass into the lymph system and down through the arm. This position adds to the effect of opening the heart and has the side-effect of releasing rounded shoulders.

SECOND SESSION – FRONT POSITIONS

This begins with the second initiation.

Position 9

The hands are placed together on the opposite side of the body covering the lower ribs.

Position 10

After three to five minutes on one side, the hands gently slide to the same position on the other side. Positions 9 and 10 allow energy to draw into the liver, spleen, lungs and stomach. This begins to wake up the systems that govern digestion and elimination. It is common at this point for the breathing to become more open, deep and relaxed and also for the stomach to gurgle loudly. This is a good sign. This area relates to the Solar Plexus Chakra and is the intuitive centre where we feel the 'gut reaction' to situations. Agony and ecstacy, excitement and fear are all experienced in this area.

Position 11

This position is across the naval with one hand on each side but taking care not to twist your back. This relates to the Sacral Chakra, the colour of which is orange.

Position 12

This is different for men and women for obvious reasons as we must not become intimate with the receiver. Many people have deep issues over sexuality and we must never intrude on their intimate centres. The position for women is to place the hands in a V- shape as the woman would do on herself on the lower intestines. This covers all internal reproductive organs.

The position for men is the two hands one in front of the other resting on the bones of the top of the pelvis. Any problem in the lower internal areas may be treated on the position on the lower back. This area relates to the Root Chakra, the colour of which is red.

Position 13

One hand is placed on each of the thighs. Some Masters do not include the legs in their teaching. They are an essential part of our being and the means with which we 'move forwards' and connect ourselves to the earth. It is all very well being spiritual but we do reside in a body that has been created from the earth and is rooted therein through the hips, knees, ankles and feet.

Position 14

The hands move down on the knees. There are many knee injuries due to misuse of posture and lack of care during sports.

Position 15

The shins.

Position 16

The ankles.

We focus on the feet at the end when they are easier to hold as the person lies on their front.

Third session – back positions

Firstly, the members of the group discuss how they feel and what they gained from the first day. The back positions are shown including the 'Finishing-off Technique'.

The third initiation takes place.

Position 17

One hand is placed on the opposite shoulder muscle and the other over the scapula (shoulder blade). This is where we carry the burdon of life. It is common for past memories to come to the surface during positions 17 and 18 resulting in breathing changes and even crying. The person is allowed to cry and encouraged to see this as a safe place for transformation to occur. Of course, if the physical or emotional pain is too great at any point we may stop the treatment for a while, but generally we allow the person to delve into the feelings. If they cannot handle it they will sit up and stop.

Position 18

The hands slide to the near side in the same place as position 17.

Position 19

One hand in front of the other across the middle of the back. Covering the kidney area and stimulating the elimination of toxins.

Position 20

One hand in front of the other across the waist. These muscles of the back carry the enormous burdon of the upper body through a posture that is often tense and strained.

Position 21

One hand next to the other on the lower spine (the sacrum and coccyx). This is an essential position for anyone who has given birth, in order to realign these bones and ligaments. It is even possible for a twisted pelvis to realign itself during this position without any manipulation.

Position 22

One hand on each of the hip joints. This position is particularly useful for the rapid healing of arthritis and artificial hips, it also helps us in our *moving forwards*.

Artificial implants seem to heal remarkably well with Reiki. Tissue transplants such as kidney or lungs, etc, are a dubious area and no real theory can be placed on it. As Reiki de-toxifies the body we must be careful that the toxins needed to maintain a foreign organ are not interfered with. Generally speaking, you will not come across this and, if you do, you have to closely confer with the receiver as to how they feel about it and be vigilant. It is one of the few areas that has no definite answer as it is an unnatural process but one which should not be denied is a life saver. If in doubt, leave well alone.

Position 23

The upper thighs.

Position 24

The back of the knees.

Position 25

The calves.

Position 26

The ankles.

Position 27

Standing at the foot of the body the hands are placed palm to sole facing inwards. This *earths* or *grounds* the body and allows the inner attention to be drawn down as far as it can go, rather than be concentrated in the head through worry or thinking. On arising, the ideal area for the attention is the naval as this is where our centre of gravity lies.

These positions constitute The Treatment. They are like being allowed to lie and rest in a warm bath. The Finishing-off Technique is an awakening, like having an invigorating shower, but is done slowly so that the receiver comes back into the boundary of their body, if they may have floated off, and slowly returns to their centre and back into the room in the present. They may have been on a silent marathon journey inside and emerge profoundly changed. We do not want to disturb the feeling of relaxation but we must bring them to a state of wakefulness that is conscious and allows them to travel home safely, feeling good. We also do not need to focus on the content of their journey unless they wish to do so as the assimilation of what has changed may take several days or even weeks to comprehend. It is an internal process.

finishing-off Technique

This is best learnt by demonstration and each student must be personally guided here to be able to learn and understand correctly.

To give gratitude we cross our hands over our chest and give thanks to the Reiki to remind ourselves that it was not us that did this healing but the force itself; we were merely facilitators. We silently say 'Thank you for this healing, thank you for this healing, thank you for this healing'. This also separates the giver's energetic body from that of the receiver if we have merged during treatment.

The experiences felt in the hands vary tremendously from absolutely nothing to tingling, fizzing, heat, cold and even pain. The sensations are always different and should just be observed with interest. This is energy in motion. The indication that a change has taken place is more important in the experience of the receiver who may feel the heat, cold and tingling too or just feel relaxed and clear on arising. Personal transformation begins in the first treatment but may not be noticeable for some time.

The cleansing process

There may be a cleansing of the system for several days after a treatment in the form of either loose bowels, feeling nauseous, headache or feeling very deflated, even flu-like symptoms may occur as the toxins are eliminated and the new frequency of energy adjusts in the physiology. Mostly, however, people feel relaxed and alert. They may comment on how clear colours and the edges of objects appear. Their inner strength may quickly return. Always encourage an early night and the drinking of water.

The 'healing crisis'

The 'healing crisis' sometimes occurs. The cleansing process is just that, but more extreme symptoms may occur, namely the worsening of the current illness before it gets better. This is not a sign that things have actually become worse but that the symptoms are moving to the surface and clearing out. The habit of suppression of symptoms with medication may push an illness into a chronic deep state, the result of which is great discomfort as the body returns to balance. In this situation it is good to encourage the person to sit it out, drink water, rest and return for more treatment. Often, after the crisis has subsided, the person finds that they are able to reduce the medication and sometimes even stop it altogether.

fourth session – self-treatment

We learn to cover the full body in self-treatment as with the treatment of others. It is taught as a quiet time of reflection and a place of meditation. We cover the treatment of children, elderly people, disabled, domestic pets, wild animals and plants.

Self-treatment is the most important aspect of the Form. Daily treatment is encouraged either at the beginning of the day before arising or at the end on going to bed. The positions for self-treatment are easier to practise lying down although any parts may be done at any time. The Reiki is always there in the same Form to be applied whenever necessary, or not.

The final closing initiation occurs. This allows the realignment to remain forever. The awareness of the Reiki may fade without the practice but the ability is always there. It is actually always the same for everyone. Some people choose not to practise but may need to call upon it some day. Trust that it will still be there, it will not have faded – just the awareness of it will have faded.

Finding a quiet place where we won't be disturbed by the telephone, the children or the cat, we lie down and dedicate this time to ourselves. Using this as a time for reflection or using the Reiki as our meditation.

The positions we follow are almost the same as for the others except that we place our hands the other way around! Give each position three to five minutes if there is time, otherwise adapt.

Position 1

The eyes. Let the hands become Listening Hands. Use this as your focus. This position is especially useful after the fast forwards projection of travelling to bring us back within to a place of stillness and calm.

Position 2

Move to the top of the head to quieten the mind.

Position 3

The jaw.

Position 4

The back of the head with one hand flat above the other.

Position 5

Cupping the ears, taking the sense of sound from being projected out to voices, and other sounds, inwards to the sounds of silence. Enjoy the peace. Remember the times you longed for this moment.

Position 6

The throat. A useful position before public speaking or even before a personal confrontation. This is the first line of defence for colds, influenza, tonsilitis, etc.

Position 7

One hand on the heart and the other on the solar plexus (stomach area). This is a soothing position for stress and emotional upsets, panic and anxiety. It is a good position in which to fall asleep. In times of deep distress and grief stay here for as long as you can, meanwhile allow your mind to reassess and refocus on some positive thoughts and affirmations.

Position 8

If still awake, we continue the whole treatment! One hand on the shoulder muscle and the other on the opposite lower rib, like a hug.

Position 9

Change sides.

Position 10

Both hands in a V-shape on the intestines. This aids digestion and releases emotional tension in the bowel or reproductive organs.

The upper back, unfortunately, has to be reached by a kind and caring friend. The energy will, however, reach through to the back from the holding positions on the front. The physical is no block for Reiki as it is all just energy in flux. Remember, it is drawn to wherever it is needed from wherever it is applied.

Position 11

Both hands side by side on the lower back.

Position 12

The thighs.

Position 13

The knees.

Position 14

The shins and calves.

Position 15

The ankles.

Positions 16 and 17

The feet. We neglect our feet. Perhaps it is because they seem so far away. Reiki to the feet is sheer bliss.

Again, the treatment is like the relaxing bath and then comes the invigorating shower. If self-treatment is practised in bed at night the finishing off is not necessary but we may wish to give thanks when we awaken. The finishing off is essential in the mornings; with or without the rest of the treatment this will awaken you to an alert freshness.

We give gratitude as before and take care not to jump straight back into our stress as if it were a piece of essential clothing. See your stress as the piece of clothing that you have removed and no longer require.

Remember the importance of drinking water.

The importance of daily treatment

It is far more effective to dip into a little self-treatment every day than to store it up for a three-hour marathon at the weekend. Fifteen to twenty minutes may be enough to start with. Each day we accumulate a new series of stresses and distractions to deal with. The treatment gradually aligns us to a state of well-being within, helping shift our ills, weaknesses and fears and, if practised regularly, maintains the new state of strength. It then becomes preventive as opposed to curative so we are more able to cope with our conflicts as they arise and see them more clearly for what they are.

Completion of the class

The Form for self-treatment and treatment of others is learnt in one two-day class. Nothing more is needed except plenty of practice and trust. This is not a practitioner class even though many practitioners may come to learn in order to combine the Reiki with their other treatments or use on its own. This will be discussed further in Chapter 8. It is not possible, as some people think, to learn something so profound and life-changing in one weekend and set up in public practice the next. This is sometimes done by well-meaning but rather ignorant people who bring the realm of complementary therapy and especially Reiki into disrepute.

This class is for the benefit of oneself, one's friends and family. If, with some years of practice, the desire to practise publicly as a therapy becomes obvious, there are criteria for that. There are many codes of ethics and conduct to follow, issues of confidentiality, a knowledge of how to deal with crisis and trauma situations, case history taking, insurance policies, and above all a deep understanding of the seriousness of what you are undertaking. There is no particular practitioner programme as such, although this is being worked on as the need arises, so assume that if you think you know then you do not know. Second Degree is also known as the Practitioner Level and it is advised to undertake this commitment before practising publicly to gain the full ability of Reiki and the full understanding of its depth. It is always wisest to ask the advice of the initiating Master who will have much experience, and will be there to assist with any problems.

A certificate of attendance is sometimes given which may be useful later in acquiring insurance but it is not a practitioner licence. It is wise to undertake the Second Degree before being too hasty in order to gain the deepest understanding of the subject.

The Master should always be on hand for the student after a class and should give out their telephone number for any questions that may arise in the next few weeks or months. Generally, there comes a point where an understanding forms through trust and people are happy on their own. No one should leave a class not knowing what they have or what to do with it.

Some people are moving away from darkness,
others are moving towards the light.

Guru Dev

LISTENING HANDS EXERCISE – BAREFOOT STILLWALKING

Stand in the garden, barefoot, feet shoulder-width apart, knees unlocked, open eyes and look at the plants growing. Look every day at how they change. From a still point walk very slowly and very quietly in a relaxed manner. Lifting one foot to the in-breath and putting it forwards and down on the out-breath and then the other. Slowing down the breath, slowing down the walk, being as silent as the tree. What do you feel? What do you see? Notice the soles of your feet on the grass, notice the quietening of the mind, notice the sensations in your hands.

SECOND DEGREE

There is a thinking stuff from which all things are made, and which, in its original state, permeates, penetrates, and fills the interspaces of the universe.

Wallace D. Wattles, *The Science of Getting Rich*

The Practitioner Level

The First Degree must have been practised for at least three months to allow a settling in of the process and an understanding of what we really have. Some people know straight away that they will take their studies further yet others must not be encouraged to book on to the next course if they are reluctant. I make it clear that with First Degree you have everything you really need: the connection that allows Reiki to be given and the ability to help your friends, family and self. Second Degree is just taking it a little further.

This is a level that calls to an individual when they are ready for it. I do not mail people unless they have shown an interest, but let the Reiki guide them. There is an open invitation to contact me when the desire to learn arises but it is left up to them. Second Degree is taught individually or in groups of three.

Part of this course is the ongoing review system so former students often join the new class to review themselves and to offer their valuable experiences for the new student.

Sacred symbols

The roots of symbolism are in ancient societies lacking the written word. Tribal rule of conduct and Divine connection were orally transmitted through myths, songs, rituals, visual images and sacred symbols.

The word 'sacred' means holy, of a Divine nature. This is very different from 'secret' which means hidden. The Reiki symbols that Dr Usui passed down for us contain great powers and unlock areas of our consciousness to empower us with the ability to create stuff out of the non-stuff, whether that be healing the body or balancing a situation.

As the symbols are holy and contain such power, the student should carefully be prepared to receive them at the appropriate time. They are not withheld from view to create a mystery but in order that the student follow the preparatory path to be ready with understanding in due course.

Reiki symbols have been published in books along with other 'channelled' symbols, but without the proper instruction and initiation they are only confusing.

Powerful symbols in our culture

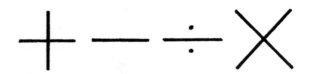

The Christian cross is an extremely powerful symbol for most Christians. The simple act of drawing it in the air becomes a blessing, a purification and a protection. It contains within it the whole concept and archetype of Christianity.

We use symbols in our daily life in many ways. Within them is contained the form of what they represent.

Mathematical symbols. The dividing symbol, for instance, contains the whole form of a process which, once learnt, can be simplified into just a dash and two dots. If I were to give you two numbers and two symbols i.e. 4 ÷ 2 =, a process of a formula would be understood and a conclusion reached.

There have been many symbols used by man throughout the ages, not least of all those that represent aspects of God or Goddess.

Adolf Hitler specifically chose from the occult the symbol of the Swastika. He took the ancient Indian Symbol of Light and reversed it to form the Symbol of Darkness. This he coupled with the Mantra 'Sieg Heil' and the physical salute of the arm to invoke the dark forces of destruction. See the power of Darkness here and imagine the power of Light.

CONTENT OF THE REIKI SYMBOLS

So the sacred Reiki symbols also contain their particular formula and process of movement; they have their appropriate place and therefore should not be revealed to anyone who is neither prepared for them nor able to make the enormous personal commitment to their practice. Therefore they will not be published in this book. That would be like showing a starving child a banquet through a glass window.

These symbols create a quantum leap in a lateral way on the level of expansion of consciousness. The essential Truth begins to become more obvious and the choices at every turn become fewer. There is a further quickening of the frequency of the student which makes the responsibility much greater, thus Karma (the Law of Action and Reaction) speeds up, so energy and stamina and eternal vigilance are called for here. After all 'The price of freedom is eternal vigilance' and it is time we were free from our boundaries and limitations.

SACRED MANTRAS

There are three symbols for Second Degree. Along with each symbol is a mantra which is the sound vibration of the symbol – its name. The name also contains the whole form of what it is and by repeating the mantra, with focused intention, the Form comes into operation. Mantras have been used for centuries in healing and Divine meditation to invoke a particular quality or rebalance a certain part of the body or aspect of the mind. Mantras, too, should be used only when the consciousness is ready for them and has been prepared by proper training.

An example of a mantra we use in our own lives is our name. When our name is spoken in a crowded supermarket *we* respond rather than someone else. It is who we have become.

We may be born with a name our parents give us yet evolve into other forms of our name that better suit our vibrational quality as we grow. For example, I no longer respond to Sarah, the name my parents gave me, as myself but have become aligned to Sandi. Our parents may still use the name they gave us, as in the beginning they helped to create us out of their own substance and thought process, but separate themselves from knowing who we have become by not being able to call us by our evolved mantra.

Class Form

The cost of this course is currently about one week's average wage. It is a big commitment.

Once a person joins the Second Degree class they have come a long way so I will question their motive and their understanding. I begin by asking them about their experiences of First Degree, how often they practise and whether or not they practise regular self-treatment.

The Nature of Mind

The mind can direct life force wherever it wishes by becoming co-creator. In the Being a sincere desire arises to become Thought. It arises from the level of Truth but must journey through the mind that is by nature dualistic, that is to say this and that, up and down, black and white, in and out, every quality of thought has its equal and opposite quality.

The nature of mind is to change itself. So the desire must be clearly felt and the mind be focused and concise without having any particular investment in the outcome. Of course, we want things to go our way, but to empower a sincere desire with focused thought and leave it to the will of God manifests dreams that we could not possibly imagine for ourselves.

Another quality of mind is to constantly doubt itself. I call this a quality as by doubting you are keeping the mind questioning the truth of any situation and thereby will not be led up the garden path without a struggle! The doubting mind is a healthy mind. However, when one becomes more connected with the Divine source within there is no room for doubt at all. A sense of knowing brings about what the Buddha called the 'choiceless path' for in Truth there is only ever one way.

Karma

We must not become complacent and think we are invincible. The way we think and act now is how our future will return to us, so we have to strive to stay awake. The Law of Karma is the principle of cause and effect. By taking responsibility for our thoughts, words and deeds we are in effect taking on the responsibility for our Karma. Karma is not in the realm of time but tends to speed up for people who are awakening. As you awaken you may begin to experience the phenomenon of coincidence, two or more things happening that seem uncannily related. Do not dismiss them, for everything that is happening to you now is the result of your thoughts and actions in the past. Sometimes the messages are so loud they come in similar pairs or groups to teach you what you are refusing to learn. You have drawn them to you, so wake up and learn what they are telling you.

The practice of the Form and Technique brings the Spirit into being.

Awakening to the Truth

The awakening to the Truth comes about as the energy centres open. The energy centres open when knowledge and understanding raise our level of consciousness, it is a spontaneous enlightenment. Under no circumstances should energy centres (chakras) be opened by someone else or by exercises read in a book; this is extremely dangerous and can cause mental breakdown. Enlightenment of the system is available to you in your own time. Don't be in a hurry to be like anyone else who you think may be higher up the scale of enlightenment than yourself. Shine your own light, be humble and accept your position in your own journey. It is where you are meant to be, but stay awake!

Ðow the symbols work

Once our thought is focused we can activate it into being. This is where the three symbols come in. The first makes a bridge between us and the person or situation we wish to contact; the second contacts the mental and emotional vibrational level; the third activates the process, empowers it with motion in an ever-expanding direction as if from within a vortex spiralling and spinning inwards, from unlimited potential – through thought – into being.

Life force + direction + activation = creation.

Permission for ðealing

The importance of permission is stressed for the physical side of healing. We have a powerful formula that allows physical healing without the receiver being present but we must not interfere with the body's symbolic display of symptoms (as described in Chapter 1) to the person unless they have asked us or agreed to receive from us with their own participation. To want to take away someone's pain and suffering is a caring act but unless they are aware of the situation their body will re-create the signal in a louder and possibly more permanent way.

Permission for children, babies and mentally or severely physically handicapped is needed from the responsible parent or guardian. Permission is not needed to send 'Divine Order, Harmony and Openness', nor is it needed to send to blood relatives but it is stressed that if the personal belief system of the relative is such that they would not wish healing then we respect their wishes regardless of how much we feel the need to heal them. Heal yourself and watch them change.

USES OF SECOND DEGREE

The two most important areas are self-treatment and human consciousness. In treating ourself we are adding to the whole and in balancing human consciousness we are including ourselves as well as all others. The uses of Second Degree are:

1 Empowering the First Degree hands-on to go deeper more quickly. This may not be appropriate for everyone. The body must be present for this.
2 For when the body is not present.
3 Individual physical, mental, emotional and spiritual healing, including animals and children.
4 Group healing and balancing.
5 Species of animal.
6 Areas of world conflict i.e. wars, famines, etc.
7 Situations – such as driving tests, exams, interviews, moving house, etc.
8 Relationships – between yourself and another, or group, or other people's relationships.
9 People who are dying.
10 People who have died.
11 Spirits – this is not an area to enter into unless absolutely necessary as spirit entities are powerful invisible forces.
12 Plants and species of plants.
13 The sending of love to our family.
14 Self-treatment.

The process

The complete Form of this class is taught only in the presence of the Master as the process of Second Degree is part of the Sacred Tradition and therefore cannot be described fully here.

We use our hands to give access to the Reiki for the person named to draw in to themselves. The symbols and mantras are used in a

particular sequence that unlocks this ability at a distance and links
the energy directly into the mental emotional level of the receiver.

BRINGING THE PERSON INTO THE PRESENT

The universe does our bidding, it always has, so we must be clear in
our commands, with gratitude and humility rather than
unworthiness. We must never be afraid of the power of the
Universal Creator. If we say 'Forgive me for I am an unworthy
sinner' then unworthiness is what the universe will constantly give
us as it will assume that is what we are asking for.

Through a series of instructions, we bring the imbalanced energy
form – the invisible body – of the person or situation into the
present, the here and now, in front of us. If we were to *send* Reiki at
a distance we would be projecting ourselves forwards into the realm
of time even if only for a split second. To bring the person to us
allows us to lay our physical hands on their energetic body.

SYMPTOMATIC AND PSYCHIC PERCEPTIONS

The full body treatment takes only five minutes for the front and five
minutes for the back, during which time many signals, symbols and
symptoms may be detected through our hands or in ourselves. It is
possible to feel the full extent of the pain or emotion of the receiver
in our own body but this dissipates once we disconnect ourselves at
the end with the process of giving gratitude when the essential body
fully returns to the physical body.

Our psychic perception greatly increases as we focus, yet let go, but
we must not get caught up in these perceptions as the Form, as they
are really only distractions from the purpose of the Form which is,
namely, to give access to another for the Reiki to be drawn through.
That is all. We can, in fact, put ourselves aside and enjoy the trust

and stillness. It is tempting to desire to become masters of perception and call ourselves that mysterious name *psychic*. 'Psychic' really only means seeing clearly. So, again, stay awake!

MENTAL AND EMOTIONAL DISPOSITION

Once the physical healing has taken place (and it may be felt simultaneously by the receiver), we give instructions that connect us with the level of consciousness that governs the mental and emotional aspects. Once we have keyed into this level with our invocation this, too, comes into being.

We call for Divine Order, Harmony and Openness to be here for this person. We allow an access to be made with our hands and keep it open for five minutes.

AFFIRMATIONS

This is the stage at which affirmations may be implanted, with permission, into the psyche of the receiver. I trust in the Divine enough to leave it up to the Reiki as, being an intelligent force, it knows perfectly what we need to be well. Thy will not my will. (There are many books on choosing affirmations – refer to Further Reading at the end of this book for some examples.)

Completion of the session comes about with the crossing over of the hands on the chest, as before, and repeating the gratitude.

Above all, we do not diagnose and we do not prescribe – unless we are fully qualified to do so.

The first session of the Second Degree course takes a few hours and includes at least one whole day to learn and assimilate the symbols and mantras.

The second session begins with the Second Degree initiation. The symbols and mantras are individually checked. The person offers their exchange consciously being aware of the seriousness of the gift they are receiving and the commitment they need to make to it and to themselves to practise. This step is not to be taken lightly.

Two questions are asked. 'Do you take full responsibility for your own well-being?'; 'Are you prepared for personal transformation?' The answer may not always be 'yes' if there is still a fear or block and the initiation will be postponed until a later date.

If the answer is 'yes' then the initiation continues. The symbols and mantras are implanted into the hand of the student and sealed for them to take inwardly. These work on the subtle energies even when not in practical use. They are brought out only during a healing session and are neither revealed to anyone else nor discussed with anyone else except the initiating Master or the fellow students of the same Form. Not every Master teaches in the same way and many have either changed the symbols and mantras or added to them. So it is advisable to practise the way you have learnt, which is simple, and allow others to do it their way without judgement that their way must be wrong if it is different from your own.

Reiki is Reiki is Reiki. As long as the initiations were performed correctly with the right intent then each has received the connection. The changes in outward Form are merely evolution. There is a place for everyone and we must be careful not to judge what may not align with our own understanding. Each person seeks out that which is best for them at that time but they must not be stubborn in admitting it if they have made a mistake. We must honour each other's pathway, learn, and move on.

The class covers all permutations of giving as set out in the list above including instruction as to the method for activating the Second Degree on a present body. Five or six hours of intense practice cover most aspects but there is much that cannot be taught until the person begins to practise by themselves. This is where the personal contact with the Master comes in. My Second Degree students have open access to my phone line for assistance and advice. They are also encouraged to return each time there is a review session or another teaching class or even to come along and go through their questions personally. It is advised that they become totally familiar with this level before embarking on becoming a practitioner. Most people learn this level for their own personal growth and understanding.

We finish with self-treatment as this is the most important aspect. This greatly improves our relationship with ourselves and therefore the way we respond to our world.

There are group crisis lines for Reiki, national and international (see Further Information at the end of this book), and also I have a personal network of my own students, should anyone require it, for crisis, trauma, serious accident or illness, operations, etc. Twenty or thirty students working together is a powerful and supportive programme. Group treatment is more than the power of the number of people.

WHERE DO WE GO FROM HERE?

A Second Degree certificate is sometimes given to acknowledge attendance and achievement of this level but again mastery of this level comes about through practice. Many people ask me 'What course can we do next?' I reply 'Go home and practise, you have everything you could ever need'. We always expect there to be more of everything because that is how we have been conditioned by human greed.

I learnt an important principle during my studies with Tai Chi Chuan and that is 'Less is more'. It is profound and guides us to simplification of our lives, to see that we already have all we need. We have life force, we have one breath in, we have one breath out, we need nothing more but an attitude of gratitude.

No matter how much we practise anything we are always still at the beginning.

A thought, in substance, produces the thing that is imagined by the thought. Man can form things from his thought and by impressing his thoughts upon the formless substance can cause the thing he thinks about to be created.

Wallace D. Wattles, *The Science of Getting Rich*

LISTENING HANDS EXERCISE – BATH CHANTING

Lie in a warm bath with only a candle for light. Relax. Begin to hum one note. A fairly deep note but do not strain. Open your mouth as if it contained an orange – do not strain. On each breath make your sound out loud. Feel where it reverberates and change the pitch of the sound up and down until the reverberation is in the upper chest, throat and head. Do this for five minutes then stop and be still. Notice your breath, notice your body, notice your mind – see how still they have become. See the possibilities. This is a true vehicle for science.

7 FINDING A MASTER

Let Life be your God. Let experience be your teacher.

Now that you have heard of Reiki and begin to understand it, it will appear in your life again and again. If you want to take your knowledge further you just have to look around and it will be there; perhaps on a notice board or newspaper, maybe you will meet someone who has just returned from holiday having learnt Reiki while they were away. If it is not directly presented to you there are some useful addresses in Further Information at the back of this book. Membership of a Reiki association does not guarantee any quality of training nor the correct understanding. The Reiki Alliance in America (see Further Information) was set up on instruction from Takata and contains a worldwide list, but beware of increasing dogma and restrictions.

You will be drawn to the teacher you personally need by natural means if you are patient and hold out for the best. If you wait, it will come to you but there are some useful guidelines that may help if you come across several Masters and are unable to choose between them. Some publications contain many different advertisements with varying price scales and contents. Your gut feeling is your intuition and is the best guide, but failing that ask questions of their training, understanding and principles.

Questions to ask

- *What is Reiki?* Can they be clear and concise?
- *What is your Historical Lineage?* They should be able to trace back to Dr Usui and not be more than four, five or six in line from Takata.
- *Do you teach the history of Reiki?*
- *How long was your training?*
- *How long was your apprenticeship?*
- *How much did you pay?* If their energy exchange was only a few hundred pounds or dollars and their training over a weekend or two then they do not understand the quality of the energy.
- *What is the name of your Master's Master?*
- *How soon after First Degree will I be able to take Second Degree and how much do these levels cost?*
- *Will I be able to take the Master's level?*
- *Can I go into practice straight away?*
- *How many symbols do you teach for Second Degree?* If more than three then question the origin of these and be doubtful about claims of channelling from Usui or Takata.
- *How many initiations do you perform for each level?* First Degree should be four and Second Degree should be one.
- *Do you include the legs and feet and a Finishing-off Technique for grounding?*
- *How many Masters have you trained?* One to three should have taken them through nine years of their practice. Be suspicious if this number boasts twenty or, as one person admits in a book full of symbols, several hundred.
- *Have you been in public practice?*
- *Do you practise on yourself?*
- *Do you teach the five precepts?*
- *How much do you charge?* First Degree should be around two days' average wage. Second Degree should be around one week's average wage and Third Degree should not be offered to you at this stage.
- *Do you take other forms of exchange?*
- *Do you belong to any Reiki organisation?*

- *Are you insured to practise and teach? With whom?*
- *How many people are taught in one class?* There should be no more than twelve for an individual Master or more than twenty with a Second Degree student assistant. Personal contact is imperative and cannot be gained in groups of fifty. Also, anyone entering a healing crisis on the course may need individual attention. I personally always use an assistant; it is also good experience for them. If convenient, ask for a treatment from them or from one of their students. Experiencing Reiki is the best way to book on to a class.

Obviously this list can be edited but this questioning should be welcomed if the Master has your interests at heart rather than their own.

It is good to take Second Degree with the same Master although it is totally a personal choice. A relationship of care and trust can build up.

The Successor

Dr Usui was known as Grand Master. Some sources in Japan say that he trained up to nine Masters including Dr Hayashi. Dr Hayashi then trained between seven and twelve Masters including his wife Chie Hayashi. Takata was the first to come to the West and so hers is the Form we follow but there are many other lineages. She called herself the 'Successor', and did not take the title of Grand Master for herself. A Master is simply your teacher and equal to you, neither more nor less worthy of life itself. They are simply 'one who has gone before' who can show you what is already within you. Never feel you are less than anyone else, whatever degree they may have learnt, just see that the teacher is the giver of the gift that they, too, were once without. Indeed, I would prefer to call myself a servant of Reiki as the Reiki itself is the true master.

Be prepared to travel

The student should be prepared to put themselves out and travel to the Master. Effort is sometimes needed if change is to be made in your life. Remember the teacher already has this gift. Masters do travel, however, all the time. So ask about a class near you, and if the particular Master you wish for does not have one then offer to create one for them. They will assist you in organising a class at which you may attend. Many of my students have done this and become permanent organisers, two of them went on to train as Masters themselves. It is a good experience. It may also be possible for you to set up a sharing group, once the Master has gone, and invite those interested to come to give and receive Reiki.

For those who are interested in Reiki but may have great financial difficulties, organising a class is a way to create your own learning of First or even Second Degree without financial exchange. Doing service for Reiki is more precious than any payment.

Once booked on a class make your commitment to it, or rather to yourself, and stick to it. Don't let your car break down on the way, the cat get run over or become ill in order not to make the change, it may be scary but remember, only fear dies.

When man wants that which he already has he has fulfilment.

Maharaji

Listening hands exercise – self-esteeming

List all your current faults including what you think others see in you. Opposite, list all your current qualities and your potential qualities if only you could rid yourself of all those faults. Include what others say about you, even if you don't believe them. Know that you contain all of this and with intention and vigilance will become more of what you want to be. You may even burn the page of faults for they are your own judgement upon yourself.

REIKI IN COMBINATION WITH OTHER THERAPIES

Suffering is a soulless state and negative emotions are the catalyst.

Reiki is a complete system in itself. Additional techniques are often not necessary as the same Universal Energy is utilised in all other forms of therapy. The others approach the being from different avenues but point the way to the same goal, wholeness. I have taught all manner of therapists who use Reiki by itself but also combine it with their particular treatments to enhance and assist them.

Complementary therapies that successfully combine with Reiki

- Shiatsu
- Acupuncture
- Bach Flower Therapy
- Homoeopathy
- Naturopathy
- Herbalism
- Alexander Technique
- Reflexology
- Metamorphic Technique
- Crystal Therapy
- Touch for Health
- Educational Kinesiology (Brain Gym)
- Aromatherapy
- McTimony Chiropractic
- Cranio-sacral Therapy
- Zero Balancing
- Polarity Therapy

It is found that Reiki not only enhances the original treatment but also has its own place in assisting in deep-seated physical, emotional or mental blocks. The release of blocks is integrated more smoothly as the energy creates a simple method of release and detoxification.

Reiki enhances the understanding of energy forms

- T'ai Chi
- Qi Gong
- Yoga
- Meditation
- Visualisation
- Pranayama
- Biofeedback
- Mai Kari

The experience of *chi* (internal energy in motion) in the hands can be applied through all other forms of energy work. It is through the hands that chi becomes tangible, literally meaning 'to touch'. Chi may also be described as *ki, prana, shakti, akasha,* electromagnetism, force, Energram Field, etc. A more expansive view is gained through Reiki as the plugging-in to the source allows an understanding to take place as if from the inside out rather than with the mind.

Mental processes

Reiki is a useful tool for self-treatment when undergoing counselling, psychosynthesis, transactional analysis, psycho-drama, etc., as the veils of personality that mask us from our own Truth, and the desires from our own heart are dissolved more easily without bringing to the present the huge can of worms that we have in our past. The past becomes memory and not a veil of pain through which we view the world. Our goal setting becomes clear and our future is re-created from a new position.

Reiki can enhance our ability for channelling, clairvoyance, mediumship and intuitive interpretation of the Runes, Tarot, and palmistry.

Although Reiki may seem complicated in its relation to all and everything it is only because it is so incredibly simple; it is one thing. It is the underlying energy awaiting in full potential to become absolutely anything. We cannot have too much life force. Once we are full we keep growing and can contain even more. The cup of love never overflows, it just keeps on expanding.

Reiki and orthodox medicine

Reiki is useful in orthodox therapy such as radiotherapy, chemotherapy, physiotherapy, hydrotherapy, vitamin therapy, diet therapy and general drug therapy. It helps the patient relax their stress levels, detoxify their system and heal their injury or illness more rapidly. The side effects of chemo- and radiotherapy are eased, including the nausea, anxiety, exhaustion and the tension in scar tissue.

Recovery from surgery is speeded up especially if treatment begins some weeks before an operation to feed the patient with an extra reserve and prepare the site with enlivened tissue. Broken or operated bones fuse extraordinarily quickly and it is especially noted that in the case of broken bones it is good to get them set before Reiki is locally applied to prevent them from healing beforehand. In these cases Reiki to the head and heart is beneficial but hospital treatment is the first option. This also applies to severe cuts and bleeding.

The recovery of patients who have received Reiki initiation is often phenomenal as they can receive Reiki constantly and probably have access to distant healing also.

Reiki can be used in any situation.

Cease to be at the mercy of the mind and all the voices there that belong to other people. Listen only to the voice of your own heart.

LISTENING HANDS EXERCISE – AIM HIGH GOAL SETTING

Write on a piece of paper your hopes, goals, aspirations, what you wish to achieve for yourself. Aim high, leave nothing out. On a second piece of paper list all the things that are blocking you: fear, anger, money, a person, a phobia, etc. Burn the blocks and watch them become ash and light. Look at your goals in a year's time and you will be surprised.

EXPERIENCES WITH REIKI

*Dance in the magic of your own life but first
you have to make a commitment to yourself.*

Maharaji

Physical healing

'A few days after learning Reiki my son was playing squash when he hit the wall breaking his racquet. That night, as his whole body seized up, he staggered into my room in tears of pain. As a massage therapist I would not have been able to do anything for him but I knew Reiki could not harm. I put my hands under his shoulders as he lay down and he went into a deep, contorted, trance-like sleep. His shoulder and neck twisted this way and that under my hands, I could feel the movements. Eventually he seemed straight so I left him to sleep. I made him stay lying down the next day and within twenty-four hours the problem had gone. It never returned.' E.A.

'Six weeks after training in Reiki a lady came to me with severe bruising to her inner thighs that were a bright, luminous purple, and swollen shins where she had fallen into some steps. I gave her a full body treatment but spent extra time on her legs. The swelling went down noticeably over the next three treatments and an extraordinary thing happened to the bruising. The purple centre of the large bruises disappeared and regained full colour without going through the usual brown, yellow stages. Around the outside was a silvery line like the outside of a cloud, it was as if the bruising had just evaporated.' E.A.

'I am very sceptical about such things but when the arthritis was so bad in my neck that I couldn't sleep I tried Reiki. I only had ten minutes to my head and neck as I was in a hurry and had to travel two hundred miles. By the time I had got to my car the pain had gone. It never returned. I still couldn't sleep as I stayed up late each night studying an Open University Degree which I passed.' B.P. (age 65)

'With Diabetic Neuropathy I suffer great pain and have searched for years alternative ways to help as the medication had reached its peak. My devoted wife learnt Reiki and adapted the positions to suit me in a wheelchair. It helped a lot but when she learnt Second Degree she could send Reiki to me as I lay in bed. The pain relief increased, I had far better sleep and eventually stopped all the sleeping tablets. I was no longer a drug induced zombie. My dear wife is also able to help herself which she needs as she works so hard for me. It is wonderful to be able to learn Reiki for yourself and to be able to help with your own family. Every home should have one!' Mr. C.

'I have suffered from asthma and IBS all my life and since the first treatment of Reiki I have been able to tolerate many more foods. I am now able to do without my inhaler except for in May when the pollen count is high, but I am truly amazed that I can live a controlled life without the need for any more medication. I have become stronger in my self-confidence and have been waking up to how much I have allowed myself to become a victim. I am more assertive in my relationships which at first was scary but is now proving to be very effective. My husband, who has suffered a lot with me, is actually proud of my new independent thinking and is relieved that I am no longer so dependent on him.' R.J.P.

A miracle of faith

'Some years ago Anne's mother learnt Reiki with me. She didn't know why, but she felt compelled to do so. One month later Anne was involved in a riding accident that left her on a life-support machine with severe head injuries. The family all learnt Reiki straight away and Anne received round-the-clock, hands-on treatment as well as up to twenty Second Degree students sending distant healing daily. The prognosis was grim. The doctors told the family that she would never really recover, certainly never walk again and may remain in a vegetative state. The family had faith and continued with the Reiki. Some weeks later Anne was able to come off the ventilator and breathe for herself and gradually she began to regain consciousness. She had tracheotomy damage to her vocal chords which meant she could only speak in a monotone. He eyes were affected and she was paralysed down one side.

'It must have been a year later that Anne came to me to learn Reiki for herself. She arrived in a wheelchair but managed to get upstairs with the help of sticks (and a push behind!). I remember how emotional she was when finally she could do the Reiki for herself, she said "It's wonderful what Reiki has done for me and my family, I feel very lucky." Not many of us from the outside saw her as lucky.

'Another year on and Anne was back to learn Second Degree. This time more mobile, able to walk with one stick, able to see, and able to speak more clearly. She had been having singing lessons for her voice and swimming every day. Her left hand would not receive its instructions so she said she would use her "invisible hand" for the Reiki. With one hand on my body I could honestly feel two! She has since taken up riding again and is instructing at her riding school. Her ambition is to continue to heal horses through Reiki, homoeopathy and aromatherapy. She recently wrote to me:

"I had a dream of being completely independent, like a bird soaring high above the landscape and valleys. Now I feel trapped like a cheetah in a cage. I share the same anger as the cheetah shows. The positive things since my accident keep me going. The Reiki has been such a big advantage. To help others that are in pain or discomfort is a great feeling for me, as I have had to take so much help from other people. I have become very philosophical and when stressed I do my Reiki and look inside, the feeling of relaxation in incredible. I am aware of not rushing but being in the right place at the right time for me. I now see riding from the pupil's point of view which has helped me to discover the need to repattern the brain for a new subject. I have the desire to teach disabled people to ride as I know the feelings of frustration and delight they can have. Telling a horse to walk is much easier than getting my own body to respond. This is the poem I wrote:

Positive love and tingling within the palms of my hands,
Red orange blue within my head and in my pain.
When in anger, my colours are bright and vibrant,
When hurt changes to tolerable vibrations, my colours seem to fade.
Flashes of blue indigo appear in the air,
Giving guidance in spirituality, and balance of life.
When in pain I feel 'Why me?', negative anger twists the pain and unfairness,
When healing I feel calm fulfilled and grateful to be alive.

Yes, I am grateful to Reiki.'" A.H.

A BENEFIT TO THE ELDERLY

'Ethne Green was my friend. At 89 she received First Degree initiation. She suffered from Parkinson's disease (with a noticeable "jibber"), she was mostly blind, could not smell and had severe arthritis deforming her hands and feet. She spent most days just sitting. Reiki gave her a sense of purpose she had not felt before and in such circumstances was needed. It helped her pain and slowed her jibber. She learnt Second Degree in an abridged form as her memory was a little short. At last she had something to do. She would spend her days instead of "sitting around waiting for the end" as she said, sending Reiki to her family and friends and even those who had died, being many and including her dear husband, Phil. At night she awoke with pain and would send Reiki to herself until sleep came. She received the Reiki Master Initiation at 91. She was eternally grateful for living long enough to receive this honour and died at 92 complete. It was my greatest privilege to teach this remarkable and special Angel.' S.L.S.

'The effect can be simple and immediate. I was visiting an elderly neighbour in summer when she remarked that her elbow was very painful these days. I suggested some Reiki, so while we chatted I held her arm gently for twenty minutes. As an ex-physiotherapist, she was amused and pleased to feel relief, but even more amused in November to report no further pain to date.' A.R.

'People of all ages can benefit from and use Reiki. Grandma, at ninety, loves receiving it. She said to me "your hands are like summer". I recently taught my seventy-six-year-old mother who now treats herself every day. Aches and pains have reduced and she says she hasn't felt so well in years.' A.R.

'One Lady whose elderly, much loved father died a month before Christmas said "I don't know what we would have done without Reiki. It is the best thing I have ever done." She gave him lots of it in his last days. It gave her strength to cope and brought about an unspoken closeness they had never had before.' A.R.

Children and animals

'Babies and animals respond well. Peter gave his baby Reiki before she was born and immediately after birth. Her parents declare her to be happier and more contented than her two older sisters.'

'Ann's dog, Lucy, is twelve and has severe kidney disease, so she receives a half an hour treatment daily. Though still ill, the dog is happy and pain free most of the time and the vet says "whatever you are doing to your dog, keep on doing it." Another student very bravely gave Reiki to a cygnet in distress even though the RSPCA advised her that it would die and nothing could be done. It held its own and grew safely to maturity.' A.R.

'I was asked to visit a horse that was suffering acute laminitus, a problem with the feet, sometimes due to too much rich food. The vet had suggested that, due to the severity of this case, the best action was for the horse to be put down. We set to task practising weekly hands-on and daily absent healing. The owner gave the horse Bach Flower Rescue Remedy and made sure it drank plenty of water. After three weeks the cracks in the hooves had healed completely and the horse was able once more to stand. It took another two months for the internal swelling in the hoof to fully subside but once it did we watched with glee as she went into a field for the first time in three months. She pranced and danced and called out as if to rejoice. The vet came to see her the next day and said he wished we had taken a before-and-after photograph of this condition as no-one would believe this recovery.' S.L.S.

fear of flying

'I had known C.M. for a while before he confided that he couldn't travel, apart from in a car or train. His family were frustrated about this, and wanted to go to Majorca for their summer holidays. I suggested Reiki to him and to my surprise he agreed. After the very first treatment he said it might be possible! One more hour's treatment and he was on the way to the airport, only to be told that there was a hour's delay for the flight. He called me and I immediately gave him some Second Degree. He got on the plane and the hostess actually took him to the cockpit where he discussed landing, etc. with the pilot. This gave him great confidence. Needless to say, he made it! He telephoned me three hours before take off on the return journey to have his "Reiki Fix", completely confident and assured of its effect. He was a changed person, plus the extra bonus of having a happy family.' S.T.

Emergency

'I was accompanying Charles on a business trip to Newcastle, a city north of Sydney in Australia. We heard a terrifying scream and looked into the courtyard of a building. Once our eyes had become accustomed we saw a young boy being, literally, swallowed by a retracting metal garage door. His arm was being wound into the mechanism but his head and body were stopping it. The shrieks were terrible. I immediately call on Reiki in an emergency situation to help and realised within seconds the boy's screams became whimpers. He relaxed into the awful situation which made it easier for the people who arrived with ladders to extricate him. They released the roll-up door and he got his arm back. It was noticeable how peaceful he was, and how noisy and overwrought everyone else was.' Susie T.

'Whilst travelling home with a laden car we stopped for a cup of coffee. On our return my eyes were drawn to the back wheel, it was completely flat. Thank heavens, or the Reiki, for a) making me stop and, b) bringing the RAC so quickly. What a relief to have Five Star benefit of RAC or as I now call it – Reiki At Command! It is the unasked for protection I think is, without a doubt, immeasurable.' S.T.

The source of all energy

'My hands feel invisible and disappear inside the person's body. They float around inside where the colours swirl and feed in light. I use Reiki on myself all the time, especially at school when I get nervous.' S.P. (age 10)

'Reiki is tingly, it makes me feel happy and calm. I learnt Reiki when I was seven. When my brother is annoying me I go to my room and do my heart and my tummy. It makes me feel good. It helps me at school with the twins who bully me. It helps with headaches and when I have exams. Even just the word is good. Reiki is like love.' K.T.P. (age 11)

'I have suffered from severe PMS for many years to the point of total breakdown. Having the ability to slow myself down, quieten my mind and bring energy in to my body has allowed me to look at things another way. I use the difficult times for learning and give myself permission for time off to regenerate. I have found that in times of PMS my awareness of truth is heightened, but I have resisted facing this for so long. Reiki has given me the strength to go forward with confidence that "all's well with my world". Reiki from other people is magic.' N.G.

'I have never had good health and have suffered migraine for several years. Most of the time I have felt totally exhausted. I began to be constantly angry and frustrated at seeming to be a hypochondriac. When my G.P. said he could do no more to help me except offer temporary relief with pain killers, I set off in search of an alternative. I tried everything going, massage, flotation, colonic irrigation, crystals, homoeopathy, chiropractic, etc. but I felt no better. A friend suggested Reiki and so to make her happy I duly went along. The treatment took me instantly into a place I had never been, the exhaustion changed to a magical deep relaxation. I felt I had escaped from some great torture. I wanted it to never end. The Finishing-off Technique "zinged" me awake again and yet left me feeling wonderful and light. Light in my body not light in my head. Today I have no headaches. I wake up feeling ready to start a busy day. I even have enough energy to cycle to work and back. For the first time since I can remember I feel alive and human. I have Reiki treatment every week and it surely is a treat. I am taking the First Degree in six weeks time so I can continue by myself and maybe offer this gift to others.' P.J.

'I suffered acute anxiety and rapid heart beat for some years before seeking help. I felt the world was going too fast. I couldn't keep up and just wanted it to stop so I could get off. I was given the diagnosis of high blood pressure and placed on Beta Blockers for four years. I felt increasingly depressed and lacking in energy until it was found that I had acute anaemia and low blood pressure as a side effect of the drugs. The medication was immediately stopped and I was left to pick up the pieces by myself.'

'I heard about Reiki from a friend who gave me a full treatment while we were on holiday in Cyprus. I immediately felt something change and on the way home I began making positive decisions for change. I reassessed my life. I learnt Reiki, primarily for myself and gradually my blood pressure balanced out. With Reiki, diet and consciousness I regained my strength, energy and hope. I had never felt so good. I cut my work down to two days per week and enrolled on a full-time, three-year, degree course in illustration, something I had wanted to do for years but lacked the courage. College is a seventy-mile round trip on the motorway but I felt I could cope with it all. I neglected my treatment and got stuck into learning and working. Needless to say, my blood pressure began to rise again as the world sped up. I took one step back and began the daily self treatments again. I noticed immediate relief, especially at night when usually I lay awake for hours unsettled. I now go to sleep very easily and awaken refreshed. Things don't throw me like they used to and I feel less vulnerable. I also feel I have something to share with others regardless, or in spite of, my personality. Reiki is always there, always the same, trusty friend. People just take it, accept it and enjoy the peace. It is gentle and effective. At the end of the day, it is how we feel that matters'. N.L.

'I had been ill with ME for three years. There was always something wrong with me and I spent most days in bed. My memory was terrible. I received a Reiki treatment and immediately the original symptoms returned but I felt a cleansing was going on so I carried on. I took the First Degree to help myself but I just got worse and worse until eventually I felt so bad I went for counselling therapy. I realised my relationship was suffocating me. I had gone down with ME on my wedding night. After some traumatic months I left my husband and am now happily married with a baby. What an awakening. Without Reiki would I have woken up at all?' E.W.

'I love my work, but there is no doubt about it, teaching and writing are both high-stress jobs. Since I did my First Degree Reiki course four years ago, I have mainly used self-treatment for stress management.

'Reiki is also my travelling companion. I frequently go abroad to promote the books I have written and these are usually very taxing trips, short and intensive. In these foreign places it is a comfort to know that wherever I am, Reiki is something familiar which I have always got with me. After a busy day of taking in new people and places and going through the adrenaline rush of giving a talk to a group of unknown people, I often find it difficult to switch the mind off – giving myself a head Reiki before I go to sleep relaxes me and quietens my mind down. Then in the morning when I am finding it equally difficult to switch my mind back on again because I am exhausted, Reiki re-energises me and helps me to focus for the day ahead.' Sue Kay, teacher, teacher trainer and writer.

FINDING LOST OBJECTS

'When my son was little he was never seen without "Bunny" his rabbit. Bunny used to be pinned to his clothes as without him Tallis was unsettled, but with him he had constant peace. One day, at the garden centre, Bunny disappeared. We searched everywhere and asked everyone if they had seen him. We left our address and number should anyone find him when we had gone. Tallis was very upset but when I explained to him and offered him my teddy he said "O.K.", hugged Ted and sucked his thumb. Not a day went by without his asking after Bunny and wondering who he lived with now. For some reason it was not for six months before I thought "Why don't I send some Reiki to this situation?" I am so used to fixing things for other people that I forgot myself. I duly sent the Reiki to Bunny's safety.

'In December my family and I returned to the garden centre to visit Father Christmas along with about a thousand and one other people. I was rummaging through some things when a lady, who had never met me before in my life, came up behind me, not even seeing my face, and tapped me on the shoulder. "It's your rabbit isn't it?" she said. She gasped and jumped back as she wondered why on earth she had said that. I said it was! I knew who she meant. It turns out that Bunny was found but no-one knew where he belonged so he was out in a shoe box to be sent to the orphanage in Romania but every time the lorry arrived in Romania, Bunny was found in the lady's handbag instead. This had happened several times. The first time was the day after I first sent the Reiki! Tallis was thrilled to have his Bunny back and said to me "Here you are, Mummy, you can have your teddy back now!"

'The next summer Bunny was again lost on the beach in Cornwall but Tallis was confident that Bunny knew where be belonged. Again I sent him some Reiki. It was not until a year later that Tallis returned for another holiday in the same place. He kept telling his school friends that he was going to cornwall to bring Bunny home. When he arrived at the cottage, instead of rushing to the beach as usual he went straight to the bedroom cupboard and pulled out a

shoe box. Inside Bunny was wrapped up in a blanket! Needless to say, Bunny has never been allowed out again. We still have him.'
S.L.S.

Even in your darkest hour I will not abandon you.

Lord Krisna to Arjuna on the battlefield

LISTENING HANDS EXERCISE – BASIC INTUITION

Close your eyes and be still. Think of an event that makes you uncomfortable. Notice where the sensations occur in your body and their quality. Hold it for a few moments. Now think of an event that makes you feel good. Notice where the sensations occur in the body and their quality. Hold as before. The first is your intuition telling you to watch out, the NO signal; the second is your intuition telling you to trust, the YES signal. Go for it, notice what your body tells you in all situations and answer its instruction. It is more reliable than thinking!

10

A GLIMPSE OF
THE OTHER SIDE

*Honour your past as your teacher, your present as
your creation and your future as your inspiration.*

Jamie Sams, *Medicine Cards*

My personal journey to Reiki began after many years of investigating the metaphysical plane. I practised the T.M. Siddhi Programme diligently for seven years after many years of deep suffering. The T.M. Siddhi Programme is a system of mantra meditation, and the use of sutras on a subtle level, including levitation, knowledge of other worlds, access to cosmic consciousness, etc. I spent at least two months of every year in the Ashrams learning the Siddhis, the Bhagavad Gita, the Rig Veda (the Book of Truth in nine volumes) listening only to the sound of silence and the Sama Veda (Songs of Truth, Indian Pundits chanting ancient vibrational sound to affect the consciousness). I became disillusioned with the complexity of T.M. and the obsession with the technique. Also it required me to not be myself but conform not only to behaving like the others but also to wearing the same clothes, no make-up, flat shoes, etc. I wanted to be just me, a non-conformist Aquarian by birth, and so I sadly and traumatically gave up all my belief in The Movement. I am, however, eternally grateful for Maharishi's wisdom in giving me a very good starting point.

In my search to be me and accepted as such, a friend introduced me to Maharaji. I was initiated into the 'Knowledge' of Guru Maharaji in 1981, a then 21-year-old Americanised Asian with a wife and four children. He gives a direct experience of the Knowledge of God through four techniques namely Inner Light, Inner Sound, Inner Taste and Inner Feeling (Reiki being the Inner Touch). I needed to give nothing except myself and a commitment to myself to maintain the connection. That connection is not dependent upon the technique although enhanced by it. It is the ultimate relationship of Master/Student/Knowledge of God. This I still practise.

In 1986 I gave birth to my daughter, Kim, which to me was the greatest initiation of all, the chance to experience for the first time what Unconditional Love meant. While pregnant I began studying Rising Dragon Tai Chi Chuan Yang Style short form, and went on to learn long form, mirror form, sword form, Qi Gong, Ta Lu. Tai Chi is a Martial Art consisting of meditation in action and inner energy exercises. It brings about a deep understanding of ch'i – the Chinese word for Ki, Energy.

I was 'Opened' in Subud in 1990 – this being a form of spontaneous Divine Worship and cathartic purification.

From time to time I investigate the way of the Shaman, having been taken through the 'Shaman's Death' by circumstance, healing at certain times with herbs, flower remedies, stones and ritual.

In 1990 while undergoing Reiki Master training and awaiting the birth of my son, Tallis, I once again took up drawing, painting and the art of 'Seeing'. I am, today, a practising Working Artist constantly investigating ways of seeing energy through light, form movement and pushing the barriers of the known world. My work is energetic yet still figurative. I have recently discovered a way to directly link the right brain (intuitive self) to the energetic vision and am able to draw the 'Energram Field' – pictures of the energy systems of people including their blocks. It is especially useful during Reiki training to see how people merge into one being during a treatment or how they choose to energetically stay apart. The body has the ability to detect the energy messages at all times. It is just a question of training yourself to see in a different way.

It is also possible to see the colours of people (auras) and how they interlink in relation to one another, sometimes even stealing energy for themselves subconsciously to feed their own particular need, or habit. It is often found that the Reiki initiation will open people up naturally to this way of seeing. It can also dramatically alter their colour to a lighter, more healthy vibration. We all have the ability to see in this way but perhaps not all of us have the need. Do not be disappointed if this never happens to you, just focus on the qualities that are uniquely you. It is the awakening of the inner eye or what the Indian Masters call the Third Eye.

Reiki is the first line of defence in times of stress as it makes me whole again. It gives me the means to hold the physical world still with my hands, to quieten the mind with its meditative quality and to, therefore, be at peace with my Soul.

Reiki is the most profound experience of my life. Be inspired, take it further.

> *To surrender is to realise you were never*
> *really attached in the first place.*
>
> Andrew Cohen, *Enlightenment is a Secret*

LISTENING HANDS EXERCISE – DREAMING OF BUDDHA

I had a dream – standing next to the shrine I had built to represent my life on Earth, the Dalai Lama laughed at me as I tried to take his photo. He asked 'What are you doing and what have you come here for?' I replied 'In order to learn and grow and to find peace'. He said 'Yes, but what have you come to GIVE?' Ask yourself 'What have I come to give?' Write it down and begin to act it out in your life.

ᖴURTᕼER REAᗪIᑎG

Reiki in the traditional form

Empowerment through Reiki, Paula Horan, Lotus Light.
  ISBN 0-941524-84-1
Reiki – Universal Life Energy, B. Baginski and S. Sharamon, Life
  Rhythm. ISBN 0-940795-02-7
Hawayo Takata's Story, Helen Haberly, Archidigm.
  ISBN 0-944135-06-4
Reiki Way of the Heart, Walter Lubeck, Lotus Light.
  ISBN 0-941524-91-4

Other useful titles

Creating Affluence, Deepak Chopra, New World Library.
  ISBN 1-880032-42-2
Quantum Healing, Deepak Chopra, Bantam. ISBN 0-553-05368-X
Ridding Yourself of Unhappiness, Barry Long, The Barry Long
  Foundation. ISBN 0-9508050-2-5
Whispering Winds of Change, Stuart Wilde, White Dove
  International. ISBN 0-930603-45-1
Being Nobody Going Nowhere – Meditations on the Buddhist Path,
  Ayya Khema, Wisdom. ISBN 0-86171-052-5
The Tao of Pooh, Benjamin Hoff, Mandarin. ISBN 0-7493-0179-1
The Yoga Sutras of Patanjali, Charles Johnson. ISBN 7224-0129-9
Feel The Fear and Do It Anyway, Susan Jeffers, Fawcett Columbine.
  ISBN 0-449-90292-7
The Awakening Earth, Peter Russel, Arkana. ISBN 0-14-019159-3

The Dancing Wu Li Masters, Gary Zukav, Flamingo.
  ISBN 0-00-654030-9
The Prophet, Khalil Gilbran, William Heinemann Ltd.
  ISBN 0-330-26220-3
Chakras for Beginners, Naomi Ozaniec, Hodder and Stoughton.
  ISBN 0-340-62062-X

The following three books contain information on affirmations

You Can Heal Your Life, Louise Hay, Eden Grove Editions.
  ISBN 1-870845-01-3
Bach Flower Therapy, Theory and Practice, Mechthild Scheffer.
  ISBN 0-7225-1121-3
Affirmations, Stuart Wilde, White Dove International.
  ISBN 0-930603-02-8

Audio and video tapes of Maharaji, Elan Vital, P.O. Box 999,
  Hove, Sussex BN3 1JA, UK
Audio tapes of Barry Long, The Barry Long Foundation, BCM,
  Box 876, London WC1N 3XX, UK
The Barry Long Centre (Australia), P.O. Box 1260, Southport, Qld.
  4215, Australia